I0156769

CHICKEN SOUPS FROM AROUND THE WORLD

By Cat Cohen
(The Earthy Gourmet)

52 REGIONAL AND INTERNATIONAL RECIPES

Published by Cat Cohen Unltd
[Savory Publications Division]

C2009/2013/2020 [David] Cat Cohen

[The chicken couldn't make it to the photo shoot and we had to use a stand-in]

OTHER BOOKS by [David] CAT COHEN

Road Horizons Division
VANCOUVER to WHISTLER to CALGARY (2020) *An off-the-beaten-path junket through some of western Canada's most colorful destinations on a limited budget. Cat's socially conscious narrative explores Vancouver, New Westminster, Richmond, Whistler, Banff, the Canadian Rockies, and Calgary. Included are 50 color photographs.*

CAT TRACKS – A BUDGET TRAIN TRAVEL ADVENTURE (2018)
An insightful journey from California to New England with stops in Albuquerque, Chicago, Buffalo, Gloucester, Providence, New York City, and points in between.

ROAD POEMS U.S.A. [Snapshots in Verse] (2010/2018)
Observations and photos from Cat's travels across America, an image-filled coast-to-coast journey from southwest to northeast and northwest to southeast through blue highway small towns and unusual nooks and crannies in our populous urban centers.

MY DESERT BLOG CABIN (2009/2018)
How the author came to build his home in a rural settlement twenty miles north of Palm Springs. How he bought his land, dealt with government bureaucracy, designed his floorplan, and underwent and survived residential construction.

ROAD STORIES SOUTHWEST (2010/2013)
Three quirky travel adventures in New Mexico, Arizona, Southern Colorado and Northeastern Baja California - **Medicine Man, Wilderness, Chilies & Hot Springs,** *and* **Amigos, Ejidos & Antojitos**

TALES OF A CENSUS WORKER (2011/2013)
A journal of Cat's trials, tribulations and rewards while canvassing for the 2010 census as he interviews hundreds of small-town citizens, horse ranchers, and anti-government holdouts in the high desert areas of Southern California.

Savory Publications Division
DIVING OUT IN LA (1984/1986) *co-author Avry Budka A witty restaurant guide to the best low-cost eateries in the Greater Los Angeles area during the 1980s. This cult classic was featured in various LA venues and in the foodie rag, The Peach.*

WHINE CONNOISSEUR'S GUIDE (2009/2013) *co-author Avry Budka*
A tongue-in-cheek guidebook to the history of whines, the whinemaker's art, regional whines, popular whineries, whining and dining, and whiner's entertainment.

Koan Music Division
MARKETING AND WRITING SONGS FOR AN ORIGINAL ACT (2006/2013) *An, informative guidebook that covers important issues about songwriting for an original act such as defining one's performance, care message, audience, genre, style and industry format. A cliffnotes songwriting course is included.*

CHICKEN SOUPS
FROM AROUND THE WORLD

By [David] Cat Cohen

Edited by Avry Budka and Karen Robinson-Stark

C 2009/2020 [David] Cat Cohen

ISBN # 978-1-61584-769-3

Printed in the United States of America

"Whatever one's nationality,
the way to a person's heart and soul
is often through their stomach"

Published by CAT COHEN UNLTD
[Savory Publications Division]
P O Box 275 Morongo Valley, CA 92256
cat@catcohen.com
www.catcohen.com

1st Printing - August, 2009
2nd Printing – March, 2011
3rd Printing - September, 2013
4th Printing - May, 2020

INTRODUCTION

Chicken Soup As A Common Denominator

Carl Jung once wrote about the collective unconscious, the common thread that ties humanity together. He postulated that there are certain behavior and thought patterns inherent in every Homo Sapiens, whether we reside in the Americas, Europe, Asia, or Africa. This theory can be applied to the human condition in many ways. There are numerous collections of folk tales from primitive and ethnic groups with no known contact with each other that contain common myths, dreams, fears, images, archetypal characters, and plots. For example, when it comes to music, totally unrelated societies have melodies in the very same pentatonic scales. Amazingly similar rituals of shamanic practice and herbal remedies are found worldwide. And as our ancestors moved out of their caves and formed communities, certain eating and cooking traditions evolved in common as well.

I won't guess which came first, the chicken or the egg. However, once any human settlement had enough structure to domesticate animals as part of their food chain, most communities have had some form of fowl, especially chicken, raised for food. Likewise, whenever a family or tribe member came down with an illness, especially one that affected the lungs, a widely used antidote was, as my Jewish grandmother would say, "Dolly, have some chicken soup." Researching this book only reinforced my gut feeling.

Recently, when I was recovering from a secondary lung infection, I prepared a series of chicken-based broths. Nursing myself back to health was a slow process, and I required a daily infusion of this folk-based remedy. I soon grew tired of the basic recipe and started experimenting with new ways to prepare this humble but nourishing dish. Searching cyberspace for new ideas led me to a treasure trove of recipes spanning the globe. Creating these marvels was facilitated by a lifelong fascination with international cuisine that has filled my pantry with a plethora of unusual condiments, sauces and spices. Researching this text only added to my collection. I am pleased to share the best of these delights with you. I hope you find them as enjoyable, comforting and healing as I have.

Cat Cohen

ACKNOWLEDGEMENTS

No writer operates in a vacuum, at least not this one. I would like to acknowledge the valuable support and assistance I received in putting this book together.

I want to thank my editors **Avry Budka** and **Karen Robinson-Stark**, who helped me revise and polish the contents of this text and make sure my grammar, punctuation marks and cooking instructions were in order. They also added some of their wry humor to mine. **Ruth Ellen Billion** contributed to the copy as well.

In addition, I want to extend my appreciation to several friends who made recipe suggestions. This includes **Ruth Ellen Billion** for her Latvian challenge, my sister **Phyllis Cohen** for her Cuban Black Bean soup request, **Karen Robinson-Stark** for Scottish Cock-A-Leekie Soup, **Candace Krause** for the Wisconsin Beer Cheese Soup, and **Michael Viens,** who felt I needed a California cuisine recipe to reflect the priorities of my home state. I also want to thank **Jennifer Ingle** for access to her vast collection of international cookbooks while searching for recipe ideas. Finally, I want to acknowledge my friend **Stina Jacobson** who had the culinary interest and lived close enough to have been able to sample many of the recipes and give her tongues up and tongues down feedback.

No recipe in this book was duplicated from any one source. Most of these listings are adaptations from my research. I started by poring through my personal collection of cookbooks and expanded this quest with internet search engines and Wikipedia. I blended and consolidated ingredients and techniques from several sources and refined them in my kitchen as I prepared each recipe. Some soups are improvisations I made in an attempt to recreate meals I had once enjoyed elsewhere.

At the end of this book I pay homage to some of the cookbooks I grew up with. Listed as sources for further reading, these invaluable texts (and one record album) greatly contributed to my cooking knowledge and motivated a lifelong interest. I am grateful to the writers of these works for their instruction and inspiration.

TABLE OF CONTENTS

BROTHS & BOULLIONS
Boiled Chicken Broth, Canned Broth, Bouillon Powder/Cubes
NOODLES & DUMPLINGS
Noodles, Pastas, Dumplings, Raviolis
GRAINS
Rice, Barley, Bulgur, Kasha, Couscous
LEGUMES
Beans, Peas, Lentils
VEGETABLES
Onions, Potatoes, Celery, Carrots, Tomatoes, Corn, Greens, Peppers, Squash, Cabbage, Mushrooms, Exotic Vegetables
EGGS & DAIRY
Eggs, Milk, Cheese
CHICKEN MEAT
OTHER MEATS
Beef, Pork
SEAFOOD
HERBS, SPICES & OTHER FLAVORINGS
Herbs, Spices, Chilis, Curries, Oils, Sauces

REGIONAL AMERICAN RECIPES   26

ALASKA - with salmon, beer, leeks, & hominy
CALIFORINIA - with organic veggies, brown rice, avocado & tequila
CAROLINA - with bacon, collard greens & pecans
GEORGIA – chicken jallop with string beans & soda crackers
HAWAII - with ginger, coconut, taro leaves & tofu
LOUISIANA - chicken gumbo with sausage, shrimp & okra
MINNESOTA- chicken soup hotdish with wild rice & mushrooms
NEW ENGLAND - chicken, potato & corn chowder
NEW MEXICO - with black beans, green chilis & corn
NEW YORK - Jewish chicken soup with matzo balls & kreplach
TEX-MEX - with hatch chilis and chili or pinto beans
WISCONSIN - with beer & cheddar cheese
WYOMING - cowboy chicken soup with stew beef & succotash

INTERNATIONAL RECIPES   41

ARGENTINA - cazuela gaucho with squash, barley & fresh corn
ARMENIA - with rice, yoghurt & mint
AUSTRIA - chicken goulash with potatoes, kohlrabi & caraway
BASQUE - with sausage, cabbage, turnip, leeks & beans
BELGIUM - waterzooi with herbs, leeks, sherry & cream
CANADA (Quebec) - with split yellow peas & a hambone
CHINA - with mushrooms, bok choy and water chestnuts
COSTA RICA - with plantains, corn, garbanzos & yucca root
CUBA - with black beans, ham & hard-boiled egg
ETHIOPIA - doro wot soup with berbere
FRANCE (Southern) - with string beans & pesto
GERMANY - with cabbage, caraway & garlic sausage
GREECE - avgolemono – with egg & lemon

HUNGARY - csirkeleves with liver dumplings   56
INDIA - mulligatawny with dahl, spices & coconut milk
INDONESIA – soto ayam with ground spices & rice noodles
IRAN - ab gosht with lima beans, lemon & turmeric
IRELAND - with dumplings
ITALY - with fennel, zucchini & tortellinl
JAPAN - with dashi, shiitake mushrooms, tofu, & Napa cabbage
KENYA - with eggplant, okra & peanut butter
KOREA - sam gye tang with ginseng root & red dates
LATVIA - with sorrel & sour cream
LEBANON - with red lentils, cumin & cilantro
MEXICO - caldo de bolitas de tortilla
NORWAY - hunsekjuttsuppe with apples & vegetables

*"A bowl of chicken soup a day
can help to keep the doctor away."*

HOW TO GET
THE MOST
OUT OF
THIS COOKBOOK

The following paragraphs have been written to help the reader get the most out of this book. First, I discuss what I consider to be chicken soup and what is not. Then I set some parameters for preparation time, cooking time and portions. Following this, I introduce the **Cat Cohen's Recipe Meter System** for getting an overall measure of health, caloric, budgetary and ease of preparation concerns, as well as the relative familiarity of ingredients. I've also indicated which recipes can be adapted for vegetarians (v).

CHICKEN SOUP is defined in this book is any soup that uses chicken broth or chicken bouillon as its base where added ingredients still retain some measure of the original chicken taste. Recipes with meat and seafood additions can sometimes push this definition to its limits.

PREPARATION TIME is how long it takes to cut up ingredients, mix, measure, season, and perhaps pre-treat the recipe items needed for cooking the soup. In each recipe, prep time numbers such as **15, 30, or 60** are used to designate the amount of minutes needed for this.

COOKING TIME is how long is spent warming the recipe items over a stove or other heat source. This includes broth making and sautéing of meats and/or vegetables before combining them and simmering them with the soup liquid. Once again a number such as **30, 60, 90 or 120** refers to the number of minutes required to complete cooking the soup.

PORTIONS in this book are generally measured to make **4 to 6 servings** as a first course or **2 servings** as a main dish. In making this conservative estimate, I've allowed extra for leftovers. In most cases, I served myself another helping for lunch the following day, but cooks feeding **4** or more hungry people may want to double or triple the amounts in any recipe as necessary.

CAT COHEN'S RECIPE METER SYSTEM

The Taste Meter is a simple rating for taste and flavor. It is my own subjective judgment from **1 to 5**, with **5** being tops. Ratings of **5** are given out sparingly.

The Health Meter measures nutritional value on a scale of **1 to 3**. While chicken soup is known for its medicinal qualities, many ingredients can be added that may stray from this purpose. Some of the more involved dumpling and pasta additions may add an element of sabotage to a recipe's initial healing purpose. Meats also may complicate the path through one's digestive tract, contributing cholesterol to what was an otherwise innocent concoction. Oils, cream, butter and fried ingredients certainly may be at cross-purposes with a strict medicinal intent. Although the alcohol in added beer and wine is boiled out, some purists may want to avoid their usage. However, sometimes one needs a cure for more than just the common cold. The soups that are judged to be the least nutritious are rated a **1**, while the most healthful get a **3**.

The Calorie Meter gives a relative measure of how the recipe may result on your next bathroom scale visit. Chicken soup is generally a low calorie dish. Yet, like a salad bar can be healthful subject to the dressing one puts on top, a soup is as slimming or fattening as the items added to it. The calorie scale is also rated **1 to 3**, with 3 being the most fattening.

The Budget Meter, another scale from 1 to 3, evaluates how much it costs to make each recipe. While no soup in this book will break the bank, some are more expensive to prepare than others. This can be due to a pricy ingredient or a lot of items or exotic items to buy. Soups with meat ingredients will tend to cost more, but if leftovers are used, parsimony can still be achieved. The most frugal soups are simply broth and noodles or grains with a moderate amount of veggies. A rating of **1** means dirt cheap, while a **3** rating signifies a relatively expensive undertaking.

The Ease Meter is another subjective measurement. One's person's easy recipe may be someone else's challenge. Much depends on prior cooking experience. Some recipes, which call for a mere opening of a few cans and throwing things together, get a **1** rating. Others need more work like sautéing ingredients, making a roux (gravy) or special sauces, or perhaps rolling out dough. Some even require shopping trips to strange new neighborhoods. These require more expertise and get a higher rating of **2** or **3**.

The Exotic Meter looks at degree of familiarity. What's comfortable to one person may seem strange to another. So let's bring in a relative to guide us in this assessment. I have imagined an aunt visiting from a Midwestern state where the culinary horizons have few vistas beyond Wonder Bread and Hamburger Helper. A simple broth with bland ingredients would rate a non-threatening **"1"** to her on my scale. Conversely, a **"3"** would be something she'd never have encountered like a cuisine from a distant foreign country or unusual ethnic market. Her lack of exposure to strong flavorings such as hot chili, dried fish oil, or cumin might make a dish using these items a harder sell. I consume so much ethnic cuisine that a meal from an American coffee shop like Denny's seems exotic to me, but that's another matter.

[½ points are used to rate a recipe when applicable]

[v] – Suitable For Vegetarian Adaptation

I have made allowances for my vegetarian friends who would like many of these regional and ethnic recipes, but their lips will never touch chicken. More than half of the soups in this book can be made without meat of any kind, since a vegetable broth can make a decent substitute for chicken broth. I have given these a **[v]** rating.

A typical table following each recipe will look like the following:

Prep Time	**Somewhere between 15 and 60 minutes**
Cooking Time	**Between 20 and 120 minutes**
Portions	**Usually 2 main courses or 4-6 first courses**

Taste Meter
5 Wow!
4 Excellent
3 Very Good
2 Decent
1 Edible

Health Meter
3 - Very healthy and curative
2 - Somewhat healthy
1 - Tasty, but won't cure anything but the blahs

Calorie Meter
3 - Rich and fattening
2 - Somewhat filling
1 - Light and slimming

Budget Meter
3 - Expensive
2 - Moderate
1 - Dirt Cheap!

Ease Meter
3 - Cooking skills necessary/time consuming
2 - Some cooking skills & prep time necessary
1 - Anyone can make this without much time

Exotic Meter
3 - Oz and beyond (Ethiopia)
2 - Something not too different (Colorado)
1 - Click your heels and you're still in (Kansas)

BASIC INGREDIENTS

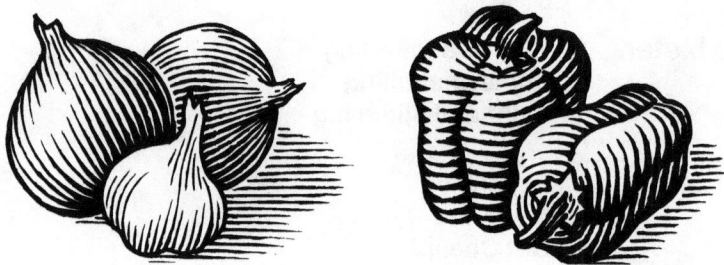

*"As any great soup cook intuitively knows,
the whole is greater than the sum of its parts."*

BROTHS AND BOUILLONS are the basis of any chicken soup. These are often called stock, and every recipe in this book begins with one or the other. Some of the more traditional recipes lend themselves to the old-fashioned method of boiling chicken parts. A quicker alternative is using packaged containers of ready-made broths. Another choice is bouillon powders or cubes for an instant, if not always as full-flavored a base.

Boiled Chicken Broth in the slow traditional manner was something my mother taught me when I was a child. She would boil water in a large soup pot (an heirloom I still often use) and then place pieces of chicken inside. I'd help her skim off the foam that formed on top. While I plied this task with the dedication of a small boy doing a grown-up's work, Mom would sometimes tell her stories of what it was like to live through the Great Depression. She made a point of impressing upon me that in those days she couldn't afford the better parts of the chicken, only the back and necks. If this was meant to fill me with caution to avoid such economic indignity, it utterly failed. Rather than being a stoic lesson in austerity, my mom's chicken soup was her best recipe, one of my favorite dishes. Not only did she make it to commemorate her having made it through that difficult financial time, this soup would help cure any colds in the family. Before the Prozac era, it was an effective anti-depressant. I share this recipe under New York's "JEWISH CHICKEN SOUP". Like my mother's cooking, it has no fancy touches. Moms around the world, maybe even yours, have been making their own version of this for centuries.

When it comes to choosing chicken parts, using backs and necks are so effective because they contain a lot of bones. Thighs and drumsticks are other inexpensive choices. Adding a chicken breast or two can make a richer broth without adding much cost. I've even made good soup bases from the leftovers of store-bought rotisserie chickens. The advantage of using meatier parts is that shredding the chicken off the bones and adding it to the soup makes for a heartier meal. Often, I add herbs and spices to the liquid, but since each recipe in this text has its own special touches, when making broth, sometimes it is better to keep one's foundation simple.

Canned Broth is a shortcut today's cooks commonly use. This can cut preparation time considerably without sacrificing too much in the results. Fat-free options are available, but I prefer the cans with a little fat, since, in my opinion, they have more flavor.

Bouillon Powder (or cubes) is another shortcut to use when there's only a half hour to prepare a meal. While some richness may be lost with this method, when there are other flavorful and spicy ingredients such as pesto, curry or peanut butter, I feel I don't miss anything. (Yes, I did say peanut butter. Read on for a pleasant surprise).

Vegetable Broth in some ways runs counter to the premise of this cookbook, but for vegetarians it can be used effectively in 29 of these 52 recipes. **Look for the [v] rating.**

Feel free to use any broth making approach that works for you in any recipe.

NOODLES & DUMPLINGS are widely used chicken soup ingredients. The more these flour-based contributions are added, the more the soup moves from an opening course to a main dish. Every culture I know of has its own variation on these items.

Noodles can be made in a slow old-fashioned homemade manner, quickly boiled or even instantly cooked in hot water. This depends on one's available time or willingness to work in the kitchen. My mom would never have used prepared broth, but she didn't make her own noodles. Instead, she cooked with packaged products. Similarly, I've used a variety of packaged noodles including wheat, egg, buckwheat and rice noodles, ranging from wide to thin, including exotic ones not often served in Kansas like Japanese udon and pad thai. Preparing noodles from scratch can be fun for those who like to roll their own, but this a lot of work.

Pastas & Raviolis are frequently used in soup. These days, supermarkets have quite a variety of dry and semi-prepared pastas to choose from. From wide linguini to fine angel hair pastas, these carb extenders help make a dish more filling. Pasta variations often add meat, cheese or even potatoes to make a heartier chicken soup. This includes Italian tortellini and ravioli, Chinese wontons and Russian perogi.

Dumplings are flour-based concoctions that make budget friendly soup additions. These balls of dough can be prepared and then dropped into boiling water or into the broth itself. When food was scarce, many a struggling housewife helped her family survive with these meal extenders (as in my Mom's Depression stories or in Steinbeck's novel, *Grapes Of Wrath*). A traditional Jewish favorite is the famous matzo ball (see the NEW YORK CHICKEN SOUP RECIPE). I'm not bragging (much), but guests at my Seder dinners have often been so appreciative of my chicken matzo ball soup that they ended up having little room for much else afterwards.

"It is a far better thing to use your noodle
than to let your noodle use you."

GRAINS are another way to bulk up a soup. These complex carbohydrates are nutritious and economical. Different regions of the world use grains each in their own way. From the ubiquitous addition of rice to the more unique flavors of barley, bulgur, kasha, and couscous, they give a welcome distinctiveness to any recipe.

Rice is perhaps the most commonly used grain in chicken soup. Although not grown globally, thanks to traders past and present, this soup extender is consumed almost everywhere. From Greek Avgolemono to Louisiana Chicken Gumbo, rice has fortified chicken soups throughout the globe.

Barley is cultivated in colder climates that have shorter growing seasons. This grain is a popular staple in northern European cooking, a hearty comfort food during the winter months. Barley is rarely seen in the tropics, as its heavy rib-sticking qualities are not welcome in soups in hotter climates.

Bulgur is cracked whole wheat that has been parboiled and dried. It is commonly found in Middle Eastern cuisine. With its light nutty flavor, bulgur adds texture and nutrition to any broth. It has more vitamins and a higher glycemic index than noodles and rice. Often combined with lentils, bulgur is a delicious change of pace in any chicken-based soup.

Buckwheat Groats (Kasha) is a chicken soup ingredient offered in any Jewish delicatessen worth its salt. I prefer buckwheat kernels to wheat, because they are easier to digest. Kasha has a nutty flavor that adds taste and texture.

Couscous is a Berber dish consisting of spherical granules made by rolling and shaping moistened semolina wheat and coating them with finely ground wheat flour. Although traditional couscous is time consuming to prepare, a quick-cooking variant is sold in Middle Eastern and specialty stores. Usually served with a stew piled on top in North African cuisine, couscous can be used in soups as well.

LEGUMES such as beans, peas and lentils make wonderful soups in their own right and combine very well with chicken-based broths. Hearty and earthy, they can be used sparingly for light soups or extensively for more filling ones.

Beans, often called a poor man's meat substitute, can add a lot of flavor and fiber.   There are so many varieties that can be added to chicken soup, from dark kidneys to garbanzos to navy and cannellini beans, pintos, pink beans, lima beans, red azuki and so many more. Like all the legumes, the thickness and heartiness of any soup is related to the density of bean usage.

Peas, whole or split, either green or yellow, make a chicken soup heavier and heartier. I have fond memories of coming in from a cold day and having comforting warm bowl of split pea soup. A few fresh or frozen peas can add a light touch and flavor as well as a nice splash of color to almost any soup bowl. Young pea pods dress up many Asian soups.

Lentils of many colors are common in Asian and Middle Eastern cooking.   High in protein and low in fat, they are welcome soup ingredients. Lentils' smaller Indian cousins known as dhal add a similar unique taste.

VEGETABLES are popular in all cultures, even among Aleuts and Eskimos, where frozen obviously replaces fresh produce in the harsh arctic climate. Every nation and region has its own indigenous crops to choose from. I subscribe to the school of the more veggies, the merrier.

Onions are added to most chicken broths. Easily grown in almost all climate zones, they are cheap and available year round. Brown, white, or reddish-purple, onions add flavor and soften fairly quickly in boiling or simmering water. Vidalia onions are slightly sweet. Some cooks like to pan fry and brown onions first before adding them to soup. Green onions have a subtle flavor and need much less cooking time.

Potatoes are a staple in many cultures. Among the least expensive of ingredients, they add bulk and flavor to any soup. They can be sliced, diced, baked, sautéed, or even mashed. Russet, White Rose, and Red are the most popular, while Yukon Gold is a newer, trendier variety. If cooked for a long time, potatoes tend to fall apart and blend into the broth.

Celery is a popular vegetable that contributes flavor to chicken soups. The stalks are usually cooked long enough to soften and disappear into the broth. Many cooks also like to use the leaves, too. In addition, a few countries in Eastern Europe use the celery root in soupmaking.

Carrots are used in soups for their color, flavor, texture, and nutritional value. They possess innate sweetness and contain many vitamins and minerals. Carrots can be added to soups in large chunks, small slices, or pureed. Their paler lesser-known cousins, parsnips, are also used.

Tomatoes are a popular addition to chicken soups. Fresh or canned, they add color. flavor and nutrition. Many dishes use canned tomato sauce or tomato paste in these recipes as well.

Corn can be either a vegetable or a grain. In either case, it is a welcome ingredient in any soup, mild enough to blend in, yet adding color and flavor. This staple is grown in most countries and is readily available fresh, frozen, or canned.

Greens also add flavor, color, and nutrition to the soup bowl. Kale, collard, mustard and turnip greens dress up many soups. Frying the greens first in bacon drippings softens the texture and reduces the bitterness sometimes found in them.

Peppers give tangy flavors as well as color to chicken broths. Besides green bell peppers, red, orange and yellow varieties are commonly available in today's markets. Other choices include wax peppers, chili peppers and pimentos.

Squash, both summer and winter varieties, are welcome additions to soups. Squashes, which include crookneck, scallop, hubbard, and pumpkin, need to be added later in the cooking process or they get mushy and surrender their flavor. I often like to add zucchinis to many recipes.

Cabbage is often found in chicken soup. Both green and red cabbages are used, especially in Northern and Eastern European recipes. They are best added later in the cooking process, since cabbages tend to cause flatulence when overcooked. Other cabbage family members include broccoli, kohlrabi, rutabaga and turnips. Bok choy, Swiss chard, and leeks are related to cabbage and also are popular soup items.

Mushrooms, fresh, canned or dried, make interesting and very flavorful broth additions. Gourmets have long used mushrooms to dress up their recipes. These tasty additions are more effective when added later in the cooking process.

Exotic Vegetables are specialized soup additions from more unusual regions and nations and are generally less available in many markets. Some such as bamboo shoots, water chestnuts, cilantro, yucca root, tomatillos, and okra are more often found in gourmet stores or ethnic groceries.

EGGS & DAIRY add richness to chicken soups and tend to mellow out the flavors. Dairy products are used in creamed soups, which are a mixed blessing. While comforting and flavorful, they add fat to the soup bowl and may not be as healthful as lighter, clearer broths.

Eggs, natural companions to chicken soups, are ingredients in dishes such as Greek Avgolemeno and Chinese Egg Flower soup. A major function of eggs lies in binding other ingredients together, especially in noodles and dumplings.

Milk & Cream smooth out chicken broths and, while adding heft, they can greatly increase calorie intake. I like to use cream as more of a special occasion ingredient. WARNING TO THE DIET-CONSCIOUS - EAT CREAMED SOUPS RESPONSIBLY! Your waistline will thank you.

Sour Cream is another dairy product included in soup making. This is usually served alongside the soup bowl as a final touch. Eastern European cuisines like Russian and Ukrainian commonly add sour cream to their soups and borschts. Latin American cooks like to add a dollop of crema to many of their soups as well.

Cheese is another dairy product commonly sprinkled on or added to chicken soups. Whether it is grated Parmesan on Italian dishes, Mexican queso fresco crumbled on top of a caldo, or hearty cheddar mixed into Wisconsin's state potage, cheese thickens and flavors broths like nothing else.

CHICKEN MEAT is added to chicken broth in many, if not most, of the recipes in this text. Leftover chicken pieces are a logical and economical choice. Since these contain bones, they usually need to be deboned after cooking and the meat returned to the soup afterwards. For quicker recipes, thawed boneless chicken breasts or thighs cut into cubes are usually a welcome addition. For a first course, this may not be needed, but more chicken meat makes a better main dish.

OTHER MEATS are only occasionally added to chicken soup, since their strong flavors tend to overwhelm the milder taste of poultry. When meat is included, it is generally used sparingly.

Beef is added to chicken soup usually in the form of ground beef or veal. This meat is the preferred choice of pasta fillings such as ravioli and kreplach.

Pork products lend their unique flavoring in quite a few soups. A typical chowder may start with a little bacon and sometimes some of its grease. Some southern (and northern) recipes like to flavor a soup with a ham hock, salt pork or leftover ham.

SEAFOOD also tends to be strong in flavor and sees only occasional use in chicken soup. Japanese broths usually start with fish flakes. A southeast Asian soup is typically seasoned with a fish sauce derived from anchovies. Louisiana's hearty gumbo often contains a few shrimp and/or a helping of crawfish.

HERBS, SPICES, AND OTHER FLAVORINGS

Herbs are a way of adding a flavorful gourmet touch. Garlic is widely used in many cultures. Herbs like dill are common in Northern European recipes. Oregano, basil, and mint are signature herbs in Mediterranean dishes, while lemon grass and galangal add finesse to soups from the Far East.

Spices add their own wonderful touches. Many recipes include spices such as cinnamon, cumin, sesame seeds, and saffron. Spicing is a matter of personal taste and preference. Some cooks like to disguise their influences with subtle usage, while others like to wow the palate with larger amounts. Spices have long been used not only for their distinctive flavor contributions, but also to help in food preservation or to aid in digestion.

Chilis are found in hot tropical and subtropical cuisines, because the nearer one lives to the equator, the more one needs to sweat to compensate for body heat. What would Mexican food be without Jalapeno chilis and Thai food without hot thin green chilis? From relatively mild ancho chilis to their fiery habanera and cayenne cousins, chilis in powdered form provide a unique zest to many soups. Hungary is famous for its sweet flavor-rich paprika, and New Mexico is known for its numerous chili powders of varying strengths. When using the New Mexican varieties, be sure to warn your aunt about their heat. Korean soups also often use very hot deep red dried chili flakes in their creation.

Curries are the foundation for the cuisine of India and many of its neighbors where chicken-based broths are seasoned with a variety of curry and garam masala powders. No self-respecting cook of Indian food would feel complete without a mortar and pestle to custom grind and blend a whole panoply of spices, seeds and leaves and hot chili powders into a curry du jour. Ethiopian food is based on a spice mixture akin to curry known as berbere.

Oils also add distinctive flavors to soup making. Olive oil is the Mediterranean favorite, while butter is preferred in Northern Europe and Scandinavia. Sesame oil and peanut oil are used in Asian soups; ghee (clarified butter) is often a basic ingredient in Indian and related cuisines. Schmaltz or chicken fat is very Jewish.

Sauces found on the shelf and poured out of bottles and cans are often the lifeblood of a gourmet cook. Soy and hoisin sauces are used in Chinese soups. Miso is a fermented soybean paste without which Japanese soups would lose their uniqueness. In southern cooking, barbecue sauces often liven up their dishes. And what Louisiana table would be complete without one or more bottles of fiery red Tabasco and other hot sauces?

REGIONAL AMERICAN RECIPES

A chicken soup in every pot!

CHICKEN SOUP WITH SALMON, BEER, LEEKS, & HOMINY (Alaska)

I got the idea for this recipe from an Anchorage tavern sign that referred to Chicken Soup For The Beer Drinker. It inspired me to find a recipe for salmon chowder made with beer which I adapted. A room deodorizer may be needed after this soup is prepared. However, the strong fishy flavor mellows overnight in the fridge.

Ingredients

1 15 oz can of Alaska salmon
2 cups fresh leeks white parts only, chopped
1 onion, chopped
2 cloves garlic, diced
1 tbsp dill
1 oz butter
5 cups chicken broth
1 12 oz bottle of beer (dark preferred)
1 carrot, copped
2 large potatoes, chopped
1 can hominy
2-4 oz tomato salsa
1 cup frozen peas
Salt & pepper

Directions

Drain and flake the salmon. In a large soup pot, sauté the leeks, onion, garlic and dill in butter. Add the chicken broth, beer, carrot, potatoes, hominy, and tomato salsa and bring to a boil. Cover and simmer for 20 minutes. Add the peas and salmon and cook a few minutes longer. Serve with sourdough biscuits.

Prep Time	15 minutes
Cooking Time	40 minutes
Portions	2 main courses or 4-6 first courses
Taste Meter	2½ - Better than I expected, but a bit strong
Health Meter	2½ - Quite healthy
Calorie Meter	2 - Moderate
Budget Meter	2 - Moderate
Ease Meter	1½ - Fairly easy
Exotic Meter	2½ - Take your aunt on a harbor cruise to her get in the mood first

CHICKEN SOUP WITH ORGANIC VEGGIES, BROWN RICE, AVOCADO & TEQUILA (California) [v]

California cuisine is based on organic produce from farmers' markets and a fusion of ethnic ingredients. So I crafted this recipe to fit the priorities of my home state. If you stay light on the avocado, you won't gain weight with this.

Ingredients

½ cup organic brown rice
1¼ cups salted water
1 cup each organic onion and heirloom tomato, chopped
2 cloves garlic, diced
2 pieces of ginger root, minced
1 canned chipotle chili, sliced thinly
1 oz olive oil
3 15-oz cans of non-fat chicken broth
1 cup each organic carrots and broccoli crowns, sliced
1 organic Yukon gold potato, chopped
1 tsp mushroom soy sauce (low sodium for the health conscious)
1 cup organic spinach
2 oz tequila (or mescal)
2 oz lime juice
Salt & pepper
1 avocado, cubed for garnish

Directions

In a saucepan cook the rice in boiling water, then simmer for 40 minutes until done. Meanwhile, in a large soup pot, saute the onion, tomato, garlic, ginger and chili in the olive oil. Add the chicken broth, carrots, broccoli, and potato, and bring to a boil. Cover and simmer for 15 minutes. Add the spinach, tequila, and cooked rice, then cook a few minutes longer. Serve garnished with avocado cubes. Accompany with pre-heated whole-wheat tortillas or a crusty sourdough baguette and a Napa Valley wine.

Prep Time	15 minutes
Cooking Time	60 minutes
Portions	2 main courses or 4-6 first courses
Taste Meter	4 - Interesting blend of flavors
Health Meter	3 - Way healthy
Calorie Meter	1 - Very slimming
Budget Meter	2½ - Moderately expensive
Ease Meter	1½ - Fairly easy
Exotic Meter	2 - Give your aunt a margarita first

CHICKEN SOUP WITH BACON, COLLARD GREENS & PECANS (Carolinas)

Full of down home flavor, this regional dish is sure to please a redneck or any color neck. Don't overcook the greens and you'll get the most out of this great rural soup.

Ingredients

1- 2 cups leftover chicken or thawed breast strips, cubed
4 slices bacon
5 cups chicken broth
1 can diced tomatoes
1 onion, chopped
2 cloves garlic, diced
2 carrots, chopped
1 large potato, chopped
1 cup cooked rice
1 tsp cayenne powder, if desired
Salt & pepper
2 cups fresh collard greens, chopped
2 oz barbecue sauce
1 oz vinegar
1 tbsp sugar
½ cup finely chopped pecans, toasted

Directions

Saute the bacon in a frying pan until crisp and remove to a plate covered with a paper towel. Cook the chicken cubes in the drippings just a few minutes until done. Place the chicken next to the bacon and toss out what's left of the drippings. Put the chicken broth in a soup pot and add the vegetables, canned tomatoes, chicken, bacon, rice and spices. Bring to a slow boil and reduce to simmer for 10 minutes. Add the collard greens, vinegar and sugar and cook for another 10 minutes. Meanwhile toast the pecans or other chopped nuts in a pan for a few minutes and add to the soup. Serve immediately with cornbread or biscuits.

Prep Time	**15 minutes**
Cooking Time	**45 minutes**
Portions	**2 main courses or 4-6 first courses**
Taste Meter	**5 - Tops!**
Health Meter	**2 - Moderately healthy**
Calorie Meter	**2 - Moderate**
Budget Meter	**2 - Moderate**
Ease Meter	**2 - Moderate**
Exotic Meter	**1½ - All-American except perhaps the nuts**

CHICKEN JALLOP WITH STRING BEANS & SODA CRACKERS (Georgia)

This recipe is a down home dish from rural Georgia. Also known as Mull, it is served either as a soup or a stew. Soda cracker crumbs are used for thickening. You don't get more redneck than this.

Ingredients

2 cups chicken pieces
6-8 cups water
2 slices bacon, cut up
1 onion, chopped
2 cloves garlic, chopped
2 stalks celery, chopped
2 cups fresh or frozen string beans, sliced
1 tomato, chopped
1 cup milk
1 tbsp each Worcestershire and hot pepper sauce
2 tbsp barbecue sauce
Salt and pepper
1 cup crushed soda crackers

Directions

Heat the chicken pieces in soup pot full of water for an hour. Meanwhile cook the bacon in a frying pan and sauté the vegetables in the drippings until tender. Add the milk, sauces and spices and simmer 5 minutes longer. Set aside until the broth is done. Remove the chicken from the broth and shred if necessary. Combine the vegetable mixture and chicken with the broth. Add the crushed soda crackers and serve immediately.

Prep Time	**30 minutes**
Cooking Time	**90 minutes**
Portions	**2 main courses or 4-6 first courses**
Taste Meter	**2½ - Not bad, except for the soda crackers**
Health Meter	**1½ - Not particularly healthy**
Calorie Meter	**2½ - Somewhat fattening**
Budget Meter	**1½ - Fairly cheap**
Ease Meter	**1½ - Fairly easy**
Exotic Meter	**1½ - I'd prefer something more exotic**

CHICKEN SOUP WITH GINGER, COCONUT, TARO LEAVES & TOFU (Hawaii) [v]

I threw this recipe together from pieces of my travels in our fiftieth state. Feel free to serve it with a side of Spam, "two scoops rice", and some of that ubiquitous macaroni salad.

Ingredients

2 tbsp sesame seeds
1 oz sesame oil
1 oz soy sauce
1 onion, chopped
1 tbsp ginger root, minced
2 oz grated coconut
1 cup leftover chicken or thawed breast strips cubed
4 cups chicken broth
1 cup taro leaves (or substitute with bok choy), sliced thin
1 cup Napa cabbage, sliced thin
1-2 oz dry cellophane rice noodles
1 small can diced water chestnuts with liquid
1 cup cubed tofu

Directions

Heat the sesame seeds in a skillet until browned but not burned. Add the sesame oil, soy sauce, onion, ginger and coconut and brown slightly. Add the chicken cubes and bok choy and saute until just cooked, about 5 minutes. Put aside. In a soup pot, bring the chicken broth to a boil. Add the chicken and vegetable mixture, water chestnuts, rice noodles and tofu. Reduce to simmer a few minutes longer and serve.

Prep Time	**15 minutes**
Cooking Time	**20 minutes**
Portions	**2 main courses or 4-6 first courses**
Taste Meter	**4 - Very tasty without being spicy**
Health Meter	**3 - Extremely healthy**
Calorie Meter	**1 - Very slimming**
Budget Meter	**1½ - Fairly cheap**
Ease Meter	**1½ - Fairly easy**
Exotic Meter	**2½ - Different, show your aunt a Hawaiian travelogue first**

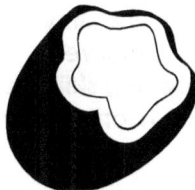

CHICKEN GUMBO WITH SMOKED SAUSAGE & SHRIMP (Louisiana)

Spicy and flavorful, this mix of fire and flavor truly delivers a main dish worthy of anyone's Cajun table or Zydeco party.

Ingredients

2 cups chicken leftovers or thawed breasts and thighs, sliced
2 andouille or other smoked sausage, sliced
6 cups chicken broth
1 onion, chopped
2 cloves garlic, diced
3 stalks celery, chopped
1 green pepper, chopped
1 can diced tomatoes
1 cup fresh or frozen okra
6 frozen shrimp (optional)
1 oz lemon juice
1 cup cooked rice
2 tbsp Cajun seasoning
1 tbsp Worcestershire sauce
2 bay leaves
1 tsp. cayenne powder
1 tbsp file powder (optional)
Salt & pepper
Louisiana hot sauce to taste

Directions

Saute the sliced chicken meat and sausage in a frying pan in just enough olive oil to lightly cover the pan. The sausage should add its share of fat. Heat a few minutes until the chicken is just cooked. Remove the meat and saute the onions, garlic, green pepper and celery in the drippings for a few minutes until tender. Set aside. In a large soup pot, put in the chicken broth and add the canned tomatoes, okra, shrimp, lemon juice, rice and spices. Bring to a boil and reduce to simmer. Add the chicken mixture and cook another 15 minutes. Serve with Louisiana hot sauce to taste.

Prep Time	30 minutes
Cooking Time	45 minutes
Portions	3 main courses or 6-8 first courses
Taste Meter	5 - State of the art!
Health Meter	2 - Somewhat healthy
Calorie Meter	2 - Moderately healthy
Budget Meter	2½ - Fairly expensive
Ease Meter	2 - Some cooking skills needed
Exotic Meter	2 - for Mason (North), 1 for Dixon (South)

CHICKEN SOUP HOTDISH WITH MUSHROOMS & WILD RICE (Minnesota) [v]

I adapted this from an internet recipe. A "hotdish" is a Minnesotan casserole, but more broth can turn it into a soup. Serve with Jello containing shreds of carrots inside and Cool Whip for dessert.

Ingredients

¾ cup wild rice
2 cups boiling salted water
1 tbsp canola oil
1 tbsp butter
½ lb fresh mushrooms, sliced (edible wild ones, if available)
1 onion, chopped
3 cloves garlic, minced
2 oz white wine or dry sherry
1-2 cups chicken leftovers or thawed breasts, cubed
2 carrots, diced
1 potato, cubed
½ cup parsley, chopped
4 cups chicken broth
1 can cream of mushroom soup
1 soup can water
1 cup each frozen corn and peas
Salt & pepper

Directions

Put the wild rice in boiling water in a small covered saucepan and turn the heat down to simmer. Cook for 45 minutes until done. Meanwhile, fry the mushrooms. onion and garlic in the butter and oil mixture in a large soup pan until browned.   Add the wine, chicken meat and vegetables and cook 5 minutes more.   Add the broth, cream of mushroom soup, and water.   Bring to a boil. Reduce to simmer for 10 more minutes.   Add the frozen corn and peas and cook another few minutes. Mix in the cooked wild rice and serve.

Prep Time	**30 minutes**
Cooking Time	**60 minutes**
Portions	**2 main courses or 4-6 first courses**
Taste Meter	**4½ - Wonderful taste and texture**
Health Meter	**2 - Moderately healthy**
Calorie Meter	**2 - Moderate**
Budget Meter	**2½ - A little pricy for chicken soup**
Ease Meter	**1½ - Fairly easy**
Exotic Meter	**1½ - As exotic as green Jello**

CHICKEN, POTATO & CORN CHOWDER (New England)

A hearty filling soup for a chilly gray day, this chowder has comfort food written all over it. Even if it doesn't cure anyone's cold, it is a great antidote to wintry discontent.

Ingredients

2 slices bacon, diced
1 lb boneless, skinless chicken breasts, cubed
1 tbsp canola oil
2 tbsp flour
1 cup milk (or soy milk)
4 cups chicken broth
2 potatoes, diced
3 green onions
1 can creamed corn
1 cup frozen corn
1 cup frozen peas
Salt and pepper

Directions

Saute bacon in a frying pan until crisp and remove from the pan. Add cut up chicken and cook for a few minutes in the drippings. Remove the chicken. Add canola oil to the drippings as necessary and stir in the flour to make a roux. Add the milk and heat gently up to, but quite a boil. Set aside. In a soup pot, heat the chicken broth and add the potatoes. Cook for 10 minutes until tender. Add the green onions, creamed corn, frozen corn, frozen peas, chicken, and flour mixture to the broth. Cover and cook covered 10 more minutes as the chowder boils and thickens slightly, stirring occasionally. Season with salt and pepper to taste.

Prep Time	**15 minutes**
Cooking Time	**30 minutes**
Portions	**2 main courses or 4-6 first courses**
Taste Meter	**4 - Very tasty**
Health Meter	**2 - Somewhat healthy**
Calorie Meter	**2½ - Fairly rich**
Budget Meter	**1½ - Reasonably cheap**
Ease Meter	**1½ - Fairly easy to make**
Exotic Meter	**1½ - All-American**

CHICKEN SOUP WITH BLACK BEANS, GREEN CHILIS & CORN (New Mexico) [v]

This recipe is contemporary, healthy, low-cal, stylish and easy to make. It's a fine first course, yet filling enough for a main dish.

Ingredients

1 cup chicken leftovers or thawed breast strips, sliced
½ onion, chopped
3 cloves garlic, diced
1 tbsp olive oil
1 oz. white wine
3 cups chicken broth
1 can black beans (with liquid)
1 can diced tomatoes (with liquid)
½ package frozen corn
1 can diced green chilis
1 oz lime juice
1 tbsp New Mexico chili powder
1 tbsp each oregano and cumin
Salt & pepper
A few sprigs cilantro and tortilla strips (for garnish)

Directions

Saute the chicken meat in a large soup pan with the garlic and onions in just enough olive oil to lightly cover the pan. Sprinkle in some wine and stir for a few minutes until the chicken is cooked. Add the chicken broth, black beans, tomatoes, corn, green chilis, lime juice and spices. Bring to a boil and reduce to simmer. Add the chicken mixture and cook another 5 to 10 minutes. Serve with cilantro and tortilla chips.

Prep Time	**15 minutes**
Cooking Time	**30 minutes**
Portions	**2 main courses or 4-6 first courses**
Taste Meter	**4 - A very good blend of ingredients**
Health Meter	**2½ - Very Healthy**
Calorie Meter	**1½ - Fairly Lo-cal**
Budget Meter	**1½ - Reasonably Cheap**
Ease Meter	**1½ - Fairly easy to make**
Exotic Meter	**2 east of the Mississippi, 1 west of it**

JEWISH CHICKEN SOUP WITH MATZO BALLS AND/OR KREPLACH (New York)

Here is my mother's thrifty recipe to cure a cold while it warms your belly and soothes your soul. May you find as much comfort and nourishment as I have through the years, as it extends your pocketbook. Who knows, it might extend your life. Mom said so.

Ingredients
1-2 lbs chicken backs and necks
    (especially when you can't afford the better parts)
2 chicken feet if possible (go to a kosher or Chinese butcher)
2 quarts water
1 onion, chopped
4 carrots and 2 parsnips, each cut into thirds
1 cup sliced celery
½ cup parsley, sliced
Salt and pepper to taste

Directions
In a large soup pot bring the water to a boil and put in the chicken parts. After a few minutes, skim the scum off the surface. Add the vegetables, salt and pepper and bring to a boil. Cover, lower the heat to simmer, and cook for a couple of hours. Strain the broth and return the vegetables to the soup pot. Serve with noodles, or better yet, with matzo balls, kreplach, or kasha (buckwheat groats).

Prep Time	**15 minutes**
Cooking Time	**120 minutes**
Portions	**2 main courses or 4 first courses**
Taste Meter	**4 – My mother's best dish**
Health Meter	**3 - Extremely healthy**
Calorie Meter	**1 - Very Lo-cal**
Budget Meter	**1 - Very cheap**
Ease Meter	**2½ - Moderate**
Exotic Meter	**1½ - Not if you're Jewish (you might consider chicken feet exotic)**

MATZO BALLS
Ingredients
1 cup matzo meal
4 eggs, beaten
2 tbsp chicken fat (skimmed from the soup)
2 tbsp chicken broth
1 tsp baking powder (except at Passover)
1 tsp each garlic salt and pepper

Directions

Beat the eggs and fold in the matzo meal and baking powder. Add chicken fat and broth. Mix well. Refrigerate for an hour. Mold into golf-sized balls as they will expand while cooking. Place in boiling water, reduce to simmer, and cook covered for 40 minutes. Set aside. Place one or two in a bowl of soup. Leftovers can be frozen.

Prep Time	**15 minutes**
Cooking Time	**45 minutes**
Portions	**2 main courses or 4 first courses**
Taste Meter	**3½ - What's not to like?**
Health Meter	**2½ - Not particularly healthy**
Calorie Meter	**2½ - Quite filling**
Budget Meter	**1 - Very cheap**
Ease Meter	**2½ - Some cooking skill needed**
Exotic Meter	**2 for goyim, 1 for chosen ones (just kidding)**

KREPLACH

Ingredients

1 cup ground beef
1 tbsp oil
1 onion, diced
1 tsp each garlic powder and paprika
Salt and pepper to taste
2 eggs, beaten
2 oz water
2 cups flour
1 tsp baking powder

Directions

Saute the ground beef, onion and spices for 5 minutes. Set aside. Beat the eggs and water. Add the flour and baking powder. Knead until the dough is smooth. Roll out on a flour-covered board. Cut into 3-inch squares. Put 1 tbsp filing in the center of each square and fold into triangles. Moisten the edges with water to keep the seams closed. Boil for 15 minutes or until the kreplach float to the surface.

Prep Time	**45 minutes**
Cooking Time	**30 minutes**
Portions	**2 main courses or 4 first courses**
Taste Meter	**2½ - Interesting**
Health Meter	**1½ - Not very healthy**
Calorie Meter	**2½ - Fairly rich**
Budget Meter	**1 - Very cheap**
Ease Meter	**3 - A pain in the butt to make**
Exotic Meter	**2 - for Jews and Gentiles alike**

HATCH CHILI CHICKEN SOUP WITH CHILI OR PINTO BEANS (Tex-Mex) [v]

I adapted this recipe from a Dallas newspaper clipping. It is very simple to make, yet tasty enough for company. It serves up well with another Texan favorite, cornbread.

Ingredients

¼ cup butter
½ cup flour
1 cup milk
1 cup water
1 can chicken broth
1-2 cups boneless and skinless chicken meat, diced
1 can chili and beans or pinto beans
1 cup frozen peas
½ cup fresh or canned diced hatch chilis or green chilis
1 tbsp garlic powder
1 tbsp chili powder
1 tbsp ground cumin
Salt & pepper
Bottled hot sauce to taste

Directions

In a large pot melt the butter and add the flour stirring the paste into a roux. Add the milk and water and stir to blend. Whisk out the lumps. Bring to a boil, then simmer. Add the broth, chicken and canned chili and beans or pintos, garlic powder, and chili powder. Cover and simmer for 20 minutes. Makes 4 servings.

Prep Time	**20 minutes**
Cooking Time	**30 minutes**
Portions	**2 main courses or 4-6 first courses**
Taste Meter	**2½ - Not bad, but nothing to write home about**
Health Meter	**2 - Moderately healthy**
Calorie Meter	**2½ - Somewhat fattening**
Budget Meter	**1½ - Reasonably cheap**
Ease Meter	**1½ - Some cooking skill necessary**
Exotic Meter	**1½ - As exotic as it gets in Texas**

CHICKEN SOUP WITH BEER & CHEDDAR CHEESE (Wisconsin) [v]

This recipe was requested by a fellow songwriter hailing from the Badger State. It is very popular in her hometown of Milwaukee. Put on your Green Bay Packer cheesehead when serving this one.

Ingredients

1 cup each diced onion, celery and carrots
2 cloves garlic, minced
1 oz butter
4 cups chicken broth
2 bottles Milwaukee beer
1-2 tsp hot pepper sauce
Salt and pepper
¼ cup butter
¼ cup flour
2 cups milk
4 cups shredded cheddar cheese
1 tbsp each Dijon and dry mustard
1 tbsp Worcestershire sauce
Popped popcorn (optional garnish)

Directions

In a large soup pot, sauté the vegetables in butter for 5 minutes. Add the chicken broth, beer and spices, simmer for 15 more minutes and remove from the heat. Melt more butter in a frying pan and stir in the flour with a wire whisk until it is light brown, about 3 minutes. Add the milk, whisking to prevent scorching until thickened. Remove from the heat and fold in the cheese. Add the cheese mixture to the broth along with the mustards and Worcestershire sauce. Simmer a few more minutes until done. Serve at halftime or at a tailgate party with or without popcorn.

Prep Time	20 minutes
Cooking Time	40 minutes
Portions	2 main courses or 4-6 first courses
Taste Meter	4½ - I wanted more, but was too full
Health Meter	1 - Not healthy at all
Calorie Meter	3+ - Very fattening!
Budget Meter	2 - Depends on the quality of the beer
Ease Meter	2 - Some cooking skills are necessary
Exotic Meter	1½ - As Midwestern as your auntie

COWBOY CHICKEN SOUP WITH STEW BEEF & SUCCOTASH (Wyoming)

A simple throw-together dish perfect after a hard day of work out on the range or stuck on the freeway. What this recipe lacks in finesse, it makes up for in soul. Use good quality beef for a better result. May this soupy stew make its way straight from the chuck wagon to your redwood patio table.

Ingredients

1 lb cubed stew beef
2 potatoes, cubed
1 tbsp cooking oil
1 tbsp each garlic salt and pepper
2 oz red wine (optional)
3 cups chicken broth
1 can cream of chicken soup
1 soup can water
1 package frozen succotash
1 package dry onion soup mix

Directions

Fry the stew beef, potatoes and seasonings in oil in a large soup pan until brown. Add the chicken broth, cream of chicken soup, water, frozen succotash and dry onion soup mix. Bring to a boil, lower heat and simmer for 20 minutes. Ring a triangle, yell "come and get it," and serve around the campfire or someplace outdoors.

Prep Time	**15 minutes**
Cooking Time	**30 minutes**
Portions	**2 main courses or 4-6 first courses**
Taste Meter	**2 - Not gourmet, but filling if you are hungry**
Health Meter	**1½ - Not especially healthy**
Calorie Meter	**2 - Moderate**
Budget Meter	**2 - Depends on beef choice**
Ease Meter	**1 - Very easy to make**
Exotic Meter	**1 - It's quite at home on any range**

INTERNATIONAL
RECIPES

Soups on as the world turns!

CAZUELA GAUCHO WITH BUTTERNUT SQUASH, BARLEY & FRESH CORN (Argentina) [v]

A blend of old and new world cuisines, this hearty soup could feed a group of hungry gauchos or a family with an appetite. Accompanying it with a glass of Chilean wine might be a good idea.

Ingredients

Several pieces of chicken (a whole chicken cut up is fine)
Flour for dredging
2 oz olive oil for sautéing
2 onions, chopped
2 large carrots, cut into chunks
4 potatoes, cut into chunks
2 large parsnips, cut into chunks
2 cups butternut squash, cut into chunks
4 cloves garlic, minced
2 tbsp paprika, (Hungarian, if possible)
8 cups chicken broth
½ cup white wine
2 bay leaves
1 tbsp poultry seasoning
Salt & pepper
½ cup barley
3 ears fresh corn on the cob, sliced into quarters
1 package frozen peas
1 egg, beaten

Directions

Dredge the chicken pieces in seasoned flour and sauté until brown. Remove and set aside. In a very large soup pot sauté the onions, garlic, paprika and vegetables in olive oil for few minutes. Add the broth, chicken meat, wine, bay leaves and spices. Bring to a boil. Add the barley and corncob slices, cover and simmer for 40 minutes. Temper the egg with some broth, and slowly add it to the pot along with the peas. Simmer a few minutes and serve.

Prep Time	**30 minutes**
Cooking Time	**60 minutes**
Portions	**4-6 main courses**
Taste Meter	**4½ - A wonderful mélange of flavors**
Health Meter	**2 - Fairly healthy**
Calorie Meter	**2 - Moderate**
Budget Meter	**2 - Moderate**
Ease Meter	**2½ - Quite a lot of steps**
Exotic Meter	**2 - A little adventurous, but not too "out there"**

CHICKEN RICE SOUP WITH YOGHURT & MINT (Armenian) [v]

Light and flavorful, this Middle Eastern recipe makes me feel healthy just thinking about it. The creamy texture of the yoghurt and hint of mint make this soup quite delightful.

Ingredients

1-2 cups chicken leftovers or thawed breast strips, sliced
1 onion, chopped
4 cloves garlic, minced
¼ cup parsley, chopped
3 celery stalks with greens, diced
1 carrot, finely diced
2 tbsp olive oil
5 cups chicken broth
½ cup uncooked rice
1 tbsp fresh or dried basil
1 tbsp fresh or dried oregano
1 oz lemon juice
Salt & pepper
1 cup zucchini, cubed
1 cup plain low-fat yoghurt
1 egg
2 tbsp fresh or dried mint

Directions

Saute the chicken meat, onions, garlic, parsley, celery, and carrots in olive oil for a few minutes in a soup pan or Dutch oven. Add the broth, rice and spices. Bring to a boil, cover and simmer for 45 minutes. Add the zucchini during the last 10 of these minutes. Combine yoghurt, egg and lemon juice and beat well. Add a small amount of broth to warm it slightly. Then slowly add the yoghurt mixture to the soup along with the mint, warm slowly and then turn off the heat. Serve with warm pita bread or lavash and some beet-colored pickled turnips.

Prep Time	**15 minutes**
Cooking Time	**60 minutes**
Portions	**2 main courses or 4 first courses**
Taste Meter	**4½ - Tangy and souperb!**
Health Meter	**3 - Extremely healthy**
Calorie Meter	**1½ - Fairly slimming**
Budget Meter	**2 - Moderately cheap**
Ease Meter	**1½ - Very easy to make**
Exotic Meter	**2½ - Campbell's Chunky this is not**

CHICKEN GOULASH WITH POTATOES, KOHLRABI & CARAWAY (Austria)

I've read that this popular central European rib-sticking meal is commonly served at stops along the Autobahn. It is definitely more of a winter than a summer dish.

Ingredients

3 slices bacon, cut into pieces
2 cups chicken pieces or thawed breast meat, sliced
2 onions, chopped
1 bell pepper, sliced
3 cloves garlic, diced
1 tbsp caraway seeds
3 tbsp Hungarian paprika
1 oz tomato paste
2 oz wine vinegar
1 oz flour
6 cups chicken broth
2 oz white wine
4 potatoes, cut into small pieces
2 carrots, cubed
1 parsnip, sliced
2 kohlrabi or rutabaga cut into chunks
Salt & pepper

Directions

Fry the bacon in a large soup pot or Dutch oven. Add the chicken pieces to the bacon drippings and saute them until brown. Add the onion, garlic, caraway seeds and paprika, cooking them a few minutes over a medium heat. Mix the flour gradually into the grease and then add the tomato paste and vinegar. Simmer a few minutes more. Add the broth, wine, potatoes, carrots, parsnip, and kohlrabi. Salt and pepper to taste. Cook for another 40 minutes and serve.

Prep Time	**30 minutes**
Cooking Time	**60 minutes**
Portions	**2 main courses or 4 first courses**
Taste Meter	**4½ - Full of flavor from the caraway**
Health Meter	**2 - Hearty more than healthy**
Calorie Meter	**2 - Moderate**
Budget Meter	**2 - A lot of cluck for the buck**
Ease Meter	**2 - A moderate amount of work**
Exotic Meter	**1½ - Who cares if it's not that exotic? I'd turn off the freeway for this soup anytime**

CHICKEN VEGETABLE SOUP WITH SAUSAGE, CABBAGE, TURNIP, LEEKS & BEANS (Basque)

This soup is a staple in Basque restaurants both in Europe and their American counterparts. I've often enjoyed this farmhouse style dish in the Central Valley of California where there are many Basque eateries (and Basque descendents). It is one of my favorite recipes.

Ingredients

2 cups chicken parts
8 cups water
1 can navy or pinto beans (with liquid)
2 leeks, sliced
2 carrots, sliced
1 large onion, chopped
1 large turnip, sliced
1 large potato
3 cloves garlic, chopped
¼ cup fresh parsley
2 tbsp dried thyme
½ lb fresh chorizo or Portuguese sausage, sliced
1 cup shredded cabbage
1 can tomato sauce
Salt & pepper

Directions

Boil the water in a Dutch oven and place the chicken inside. Lower the heat and skim the foam off the top. Cover and simmer for an hour. Remove the chicken to cool. Add the beans, vegetables and herbs to the broth and simmer 20 more minutes. Meanwhile, in a frying pan cook the sausage over a medium heat until no longer pink. Drain on paper towels and add to the soup. Remove the chicken meat from the bones, shred and add to the broth along with the cabbage and tomato sauce. Cook for 10 minutes and serve.

Prep Time	**35 minutes**
Cooking Time	**90 minutes**
Portions	**3-4 main courses or 6-8 first courses**
Taste Meter	**4½ - A tasty blend of flavors that only gets better when stored in the fridge to age a bit**
Health Meter	**2 - Moderately healthy**
Calorie Meter	**2 - Moderate**
Budget Meter	**2 - Moderate cost**
Ease Meter	**2 - A moderate amount of work**
Exotic Meter	**2 - A nice change of pace**

WATERZOOI WITH LEEKS, HERBS, SHERRY, & CREAM (Belgium) [v]

From the North Belgian town of Ghent, this recipe is an elegant, very rich soup popular with Flemish diners. Extremely filling, it is probably better suited to small portions as a first course. If you insist on making a whole meal of this dish, don't say I didn't warn you. I wouldn't go for some French pastry afterwards. You may have to waddle out of the room or call for some assistance.

Ingredients

2 medium onions, chopped
3 carrots, finely chopped
3 large leeks, thinly sliced
2 large potatoes, diced
2 tbsp butter
6 cups chicken broth
1 bouquet garni (tied up fresh bay leaves, thyme and parsley)
2-4 oz dry sherry
2 cups leftover chicken meat or cut-up thawed breasts and thighs
1 egg, beaten
1 cup heavy cream (or half 'n half, no 2% milk allowed)

Directions

Saute the vegetables in butter in a large soup pan or Dutch oven for a few minutes until tender. Add the broth and bouquet garni, bring to a boil, cover the pot, and simmer for 20 minutes. Add the sherry and chicken meat, cooking another 20 minutes or so. Beat the egg and fold in the cream. Add a small amount of broth at a time to temper this. Slowly add to the soup, stirring and simmering a couple of minutes more. Remove the bouquet garni and serve with a crusty French bread or baguette.

Prep Time	**20 minutes**
Cooking Time	**50 minutes**
Portions	**2 main courses or 4 first courses**
Taste Meter	**4½ - Gourmet flavor, but very filling**
Health Meter	**1½ - Hearty more than healthy**
Calorie Meter	**3 - Off the charts!**
Budget Meter	**2½ - Fairly expensive for soup**
Ease Meter	**2 - Moderate**
Exotic Meter	**2 - Not your aunt's chicken soup unless she's Belgian**

CHICKEN SOUP WITH SPLIT YELLOW PEAS & A HAMBONE (Canada - Quebec)

A very hearty soup, this recipe is Quebec's signature dish, just what one would expect in a cold climate cuisine. Come inside from the frigid weather and warm yourself with this down home filling meal.

Ingredients

2 cups split yellow peas
2 slices bacon, cut up
3 celery ribs, chopped
1 large onion, chopped
2 carrots, chopped
3 cloves garlic, diced
6 cups chicken broth
1 hambone or ham hock
2 bay leaves
1 tbsp fresh or dried thyme
1 tbsp poultry seasoning
1 oz vinegar
1 tbsp sugar

Directions

Pre-soak the split peas for an hour. Drain. Fry the bacon in a large soup pot or Dutch oven. Add the vegetables and sauté briefly in the drippings. Add the broth, split peas, hambone and spices. Bring to boil, cover and simmer for an hour, stirring occasionally. Remove the hambone, cool, and take the meat off the bone. Return to the soup and cook another 20 minutes. Add the vinegar and sugar near the end of the cooking time. Serve with home baked dinner rolls.

Prep Time	**15 minutes**
Cooking Time	**90 minutes**
Portions	**3 main courses or 6-8 first courses**
Taste Meter	**4 - Ham and peas override the broth, but who cares**
Health Meter	**2½ - Not the healthiest, but good**
Calorie Meter	**2½ - Fairly rich**
Budget Meter	**1½ - Moderate**
Ease Meter	**2 - A bit of work, but not too much**
Exotic Meter	**1½ - As unusual as snow in a Canadian winter**

CHICKEN SOUP WITH MUSHROOMS, BOK CHOY, & WATER CHESTNUTS (China) [v]

Coming up with only one chicken soup from our planet's most populous nation was a real challenge. China has so many diverse regions and styles of cooking that I combined several recipes into one, adding several Asian vegetables found in most grocery stores.

Ingredients

1 cup cooked chicken leftovers or thawed breasts or thighs, cubed
1 tbsp each sesame oil and chili oil
3 tbsp minced ginger root
1 onion, sliced finely
4 fresh mushrooms (Shitake or regular), sliced
3 cans chicken broth
2 oz soy sauce
1 oz rice wine or dry sherry
1 tsp chili-garlic sauce
1 small can sliced water chestnuts
1 can baby corn
2 cups sliced bok choy
1 cup fresh pea pods with the strings removed
1-2 cups pre-cooked wheat or rice noodles
2 green onions, chopped

Directions

Cut the chicken into small cubes and saute for few minutes in a large soup pot with the oils and remove. Fry the ginger root, onion, and mushrooms in the remaining oil until soft. Return the chicken and cook another minute. Turn off the heat and let the flavors mellow a few minutes. Add the broth, wine and sauces and heat until the liquid boils. Reduce to simmer and add the water chestnuts, peapods, and green onions. Cook a few more minutes. Add the noodles and serve immediately. Optional ingredients added at the last minute include cubed tofu, thinly sliced green onions, bean sprouts and barbecue pork slices.

Prep Time	**15 minutes**
Cooking Time	**30 minutes**
Portions	**2 main courses or 4 first courses**
Taste Meter	**3½ - Tasty**
Health Meter	**3 - Very healthy**
Calorie Meter	**1 - Very slimming**
Budget Meter	**1½ - Fairly inexpensive**
Ease Meter	**1½ - Very easy to make**
Exotic Meter	**1 - if you're Chinese or Jewish, 2 if you're not**

CHICKEN SOUP WITH PLANTAINS, CORN, GARBANZOS & YUCCA ROOT (Costa Rica) [v]

Plantains (thick, starchy bananas) are a staple in Central America, and they make a welcome addition to this basic chicken soup recipe. So does another starch from the tropics, yucca root.

Ingredients

1 tbsp olive oil
1 onion, chopped
2 cloves garlic, diced
1 oz olive oil
2 carrots, chopped
2 celery ribs, chopped
6 cups chicken broth
2 green plantains, peeled, quartered and thinly sliced
3 ears corn on the cob, quartered
1 can garbanzo beans
1 cup diced yucca root
½ cup cilantro, finely diced
1 oz lime juice
1 tsp each powdered chili and cumin
Salt & pepper

Directions

Saute the onion, garlic, carrots, and celery in enough oil to lightly cover a large soup pan. Stir for a few minutes, then add the broth and bring to a boil. Lower the heat and add the plantains, corn, garbanzos, yucca root and cilantro. Add the chicken broth, lime juice and spices. Bring to a boil, then reduce heat and simmer uncovered for 40 minutes. Garnish with more cilantro.

Prep Time	**15 minutes**
Cooking Time	**30 minutes**
Portions	**2 main courses or 4 first courses**
Taste Meter	**3 - Tasty variation of a basic dish**
Health Meter	**2 - Fairly healthy**
Calorie Meter	**2½ - Fairly rich**
Budget Meter	**2 - Moderately cheap**
Ease Meter	**1½ - Very easy to make**
Exotic Meter	**2½ - Different, but hardly life changing**

CHICKEN SOUP WITH BLACK BEANS, HAM & HARD-BOILED EGG (Cuba)

A popular staple in Cuban restaurants, this recipe is an adaptation of one I found from the Bonita Café in Brooklyn. A streamlined version uses canned black beans. if you enjoy a stronger flavor, be sure to make it the longer traditional way.

Ingredients

1½ cups dry black beans, pre-soaked
6 cups water
*(easier version uses 2 15-oz cans black beans with liquid)
¼ pound ham, cubed (optional)
3 tbsp olive oil
2 medium onions, chopped
1 bell pepper, green or red, chopped
4 cloves garlic, minced
2 tbsp cumin
1tbsp each oregano and powdered chili
2 bay leaves
4 cups chicken stock
Juice of 1 lime
Salt & pepper
2 hard-boiled eggs, crumbled

Directions

For the long version, put the beans in boiling water, then turn off the heat. Let soak for a few hours depending on your time frame. Drain and discard debris if any. Boil the water, return the beans to the pot, add the ham, if desired, cover, and simmer for 1½ hours. Set aside. In another soup pot, saute the onions, garlic, and bell pepper in the olive oil until tender. Stir in the spices, add the stock, cooked (or canned) beans with liquid, salt and pepper, and simmer another 20 minutes. Remove the bay leaves. Meanwhile, boil the eggs for 10 minutes, cool, peel and shred. Take one half of the soup and put this in a blender for a short while, then return to the soup pot for a creamier texture. Serve the soup with egg on top.

Prep Time	15 or 30 minutes
Cooking Time	30 or 120 minutes
Portions	3-4 main courses or 6-8 first courses
Taste Meter	5 - A rave review
Health Meter	2 - Fairly healthy
Calorie Meter	2½ - Fairly rich
Budget Meter	2 - Moderate
Ease Meter	*2½ - Traditional or 1½ - Quick version
Exotic Meter	1 - For Floridians, 2 for others

DORO WOT SOUP WITH BERBERE (Ethiopia)

This is my soupy adaptation of a popular Ethiopian stew. It is spicy as all get out and usually served with injera, a sour crepe-like bread made with tef, a grain similar to buckwheat. I'll omit the crepe-making, because tef is hard to find. If you don't have an Ethiopian market nearby, try substituting another sour bread.

Ingredients

4-6 chicken thighs and/or drumsticks
Juice of 1 lemon in a bowl of water
2 oz. butter, clarified if possible
2 onions, very finely chopped
2 cloves garlic, diced
2 tbsp diced ginger root
2 oz berbere (see below)
2 oz tomato paste
6 cups chicken broth
½ cup white rice
1 cup frozen okra

Directions

Pre-soak the chicken pieces in a bowl of lemon water for 30 minutes. Meanwhile, in a soup pot sauté the onions, garlic and ginger root in the butter for a few minutes. Blend the berbere mixture and tomato paste into the butter. Add the chicken broth and bring to a boil, then simmer a few more minutes. Remove the chicken pieces from the water and place them and the rice and okra in the broth, cooking another 15 minutes. DO NOT OVERCOOK THE OKRA! Serve with steamed collard greens and injera.

Prep Time	**30 minutes**
Cooking Time	**30 minutes**
Portions	**2 main courses or 4 first courses**
Taste Meter	**4½ - Spicy, flavorful and sensual**
Health Meter	**2 - Fairly healthy**
Calorie Meter	**2 - Moderate**
Budget Meter	**2 - Moderately inexpensive**
Ease Meter	**2½ - A fair amount of work**
Exotic Meter	**3 - Hoo Boy!**

BERBERE
Ingredients
2 tbsp ground ginger
1 tsp ground turmeric
1 tsp ground coriander
1 tsp ground cardamom
1 tsp ground fenugreek
1 tsp ground cinnamon
1 tsp ground cumin
1 tsp allspice
½ tsp ground cloves
2 tbsp cayenne or other hot powdered chili pepper
2 tbsp ground sweet Hungarian paprika
2 tbsp salt
1 tsp ground pepper

Directions
In a heavy iron skillet toast the spices over a low heat for 4 to 5 minutes. Add the paprika, powdered chili, salt and pepper, and continue toasting another 10 minutes.   Store in a container in the refrigerator for later use.

Prep Time	5 minutes
Cooking Time	15 minutes
Portions	Enough for several meals
Taste Meter	4½ - Ethiopia's version of Jack's secret sauce
Health Meter	2 - Fairly healthy if you can stand the heat
Calorie Meter	2 – Not fattening
Budget Meter	2 - Moderately inexpensive
Ease Meter	2 - A fair amount of work
Exotic Meter	3 - Hoo Boy!

POTAGE AU PISTOU (Southern France) [v]

How did we ever live before fresh basil was discovered? Pistou is French for the Italian word pesto, a recent favorite in the U.S. This soup packs a lot of pleasure for the little time invested in preparing it. I'll make a pesto of myself for this dish anytime.

Ingredients
1 cup boneless chicken meat, cut into ½ inch pieces
1 onion, sliced finely
3 cloves garlic, chopped
1 oz olive oil
6 cups chicken broth
1 can diced tomatoes
1 can great northern or similar beans
2 medium carrots
1 large potato, diced
1 cup frozen Italian green beans
1 oz lemon juice
1 tsp each tarragon and oregano, optional
Salt & pepper
Grated Parmesan or Romano cheese to taste

Pistou (Pesto) Ingredients
3 oz olive oil
3 cloves garlic
¼ cup pine or other nuts
¼ cup grated Parmesan or Romano cheese
½ cup basil leaves

Directions
Saute the chicken in a soup pot with the onion and garlic in olive oil until brown. Add the broth and bring to a slow boil. Add the tomatoes, beans, vegetables, lemon juice and spices. Simmer for 20 minutes. Serve with the pistou and more grated cheese. For the pistou, put the ingredients in a blender or food processor and mix slightly until smooth. Add to the soup just before serving.

Prep Time	**25 minutes**
Cooking Time	**30 minutes**
Portions	**2 main courses or 4-6 first courses**
Taste Meter	**4½ - A tasty treat**
Health Meter	**2½ - Very healthy**
Calorie Meter	**1½ - Fairly low-cal**
Budget Meter	**1½ - Fairly cheap**
Ease Meter	**2½ - Some cooking skills necessary**
Exotic Meter	**2 - Have your aunt watch the food news cable channel first**

CHICKEN SOUP WITH CABBAGE, CARAWAY & GARLIC SAUSAGE (Germany)

This is a traditional German soup flavored with caraway and celery seeds. Easy to make, when served with the right beer it can turn any month into an Oktoberfestive occasion.

Ingredients

1 onion, sliced finely
2 cloves garlic, chopped
1 oz unsalted butter
10 cups chicken broth
2 large potato, diced
2 medium carrots, sliced
1 kohlrabi, cubed
½ cup parsley, minced
1 tbsp each caraway and celery seeds
½ lb garlic sausage, cut into ½ inch rounds
1 lb boneless chicken meat, cut into small pieces
½ head large green cabbage, cored and finely shredded
Salt & pepper

Directions

Saute the onion and garlic in butter in the bottom of a large soup pot. Add the chicken broth, potatoes, carrots, kohlrabi, parsley, caraway and celery seeds and sausage. Bring to a slow boil over a high heat, then reduce heat and cook 15 minutes. Add the chicken meat and cabbage. Cover and simmer for 10-15 minutes, stirring occasionally. DO NOT OVERCOOK THE CABBAGE! Serve with a fine German beer (or two) and pumpernickel bread.

Prep Time	**15 minutes**
Cooking Time	**30 minutes**
Portions	**2 main courses or 4-6 first courses**
Taste Meter	**4 - Wonderful caraway and celery seed flavor**
Health Meter	**2½ - Moderately healthy**
Calorie Meter	**2 - Moderate**
Budget Meter	**2 - Moderate**
Ease Meter	**1½ - Not much cooking skill necessary**
Exotic Meter	**1½ - With all the Germans in the Midwest, not very exotic to most aunts**

AVGOLEMONO CHICKEN SOUP (Greece) [v]

A Greek friend once served me this soup as a first course at a midnight meal after Eastern Orthodox Easter services. It is so light you could float up towards the heavens after consuming it. After a second or third helping (to the consternation of my ancestors) I might even convert over this dish.

Ingredients

6 cups chicken broth
½ cup white rice
1 tsp oregano
1 tsp paprika
1 tbsp olive oil
2 oz lemon juice
Salt & pepper
3 eggs, beaten

Directions

Put the chicken broth into a soup pot and bring to a slow boil. Add the rice and herbs, cover, lower the heat, and simmer for 20 minutes. When this is almost finished, beat the eggs in a bowl with the olive oil and lemon juice until thick. Add a small amount of hot soup to the eggs to temper the eggs. Add this mixture gradually to the soup as well as the spices. Bring almost to a boil, simmer until thickened, and serve immediately.

Prep Time	**15 minutes**
Cooking Time	**30 minutes**
Portions	**2 main courses or 4-6 first courses**
Taste Meter	**4½ - Wonderful and smooth**
Health Meter	**2½ - Very healthy**
Calorie Meter	**1½ - Fairly low-cal**
Budget Meter	**1½ - Fairly cheap**
Ease Meter	**1½ - Very easy to make**
Exotic Meter	**2 - Different, but not a feather ruffler**

CSIRKELVES WITH LIVER DUMPLINGS (Hungary)

From the plains of Central Europe to your kitchen, this old world recipe is basic and fail-safe. Make sure to use fresh high quality paprika from the old country for a better result. The dumplings required some practice. I needed a couple of tries to get them right. (Thank God for matzo balls. I didn't need too much practice.)

Ingredients

1 large fryer or several thawed breasts or thighs cut into pieces
8 cups cold water
1 tbsp salt
1 tbsp black pepper
2 tbsp Hungarian paprika
¼ tsp mace (if available)
3 large carrots, sliced
3 potatoes, sliced
½ small head of cabbage, in wedges
1 kohlrabi, cubed
1 onion, chopped
2 cloves garlic, diced
1 bunch of parsley, tied in a bunch

Directions

Place the fryer pieces in water in a large pot. Bring the liquid to a boil and scoop off the foam that develops. Add salt, pepper and paprika and simmer covered for 40 minutes. Add the vegetables and herbs. Continue to simmer another 20 minutes until tender. Remove the parsley and the chicken. Shred the meat off the bones and place the chicken meat back in the soup pot. Add the dumplings just before serving.

Prep Time	**15 minutes**
Cooking Time	**60 minutes**
Portions	**4 main courses or 6-8 first courses**
Taste Meter	**3 - I was given some paprika from Hungary which made a big difference**
Health Meter	**2 - Fairly healthy**
Calorie Meter	**2 - Moderate**
Budget Meter	**2 - Moderate**
Ease Meter	**2 – Moderate**
Exotic Meter	**2 – Familiar, yet has a bit of zing**

LIVER DUMPLINGS
Ingredients
2-4 chicken livers
4 sprigs parsley
1 onion
2 cups all-purpose flour
1 tsp grated nutmeg
1 tsp each salt and pepper
¼ cup milk
3 eggs
Directions
Combine the liver, parsley, onion, eggs, flour, nutmeg, salt and pepper in a food processor or blender. Drop by tiny spoonfuls into boiling water. Cook for 10-15 minutes until they float to the top. Drain and transfer the dumplings to the soup.

Prep Time	**15 minutes**
Cooking Time	**10 minutes**
Portions	**2 main courses or 4 first courses**
Taste Meter	**3 - Unique subtle liver flavor**
Health Meter	**2½ - Not the most healthful (if you read up on organ meats)**
Calorie Meter	**2½ - Very filling**
Budget Meter	**1½ - Fairly inexpensive**
Ease Meter	**2 - Some cooking skills are needed**
Exotic Meter	**2 - Liver and nutmeg add some distinction. For your aunt's sake, go easy on the chicken livers!**

"Ask not what your soup can do for your dumpling, but instead what your dumpling can do for your soup."

MULLIGATAWNY WITH DAHL, SPICES & COCONUT MILK (India) [v]

Mulligatawny ranges from mild to fiery versions. This recipe is easy to make and somewhere in the middle.

Ingredients

1 large onion, chopped very fine
1 potato, sliced into small pieces
1 carrot, sliced finely
1 medium zucchini
4 cloves garlic, diced
1 tbsp each turmeric and garam masala (Indian spice powder)
1 tsp each cinnamon, ground cumin & powdered coriander
1 tsp chili powder (pick your heat level)
½ tsp freshly grated or powdered nutmeg
1 oz each canola oil and butter, clarified if possible
1-2 cups thawed chicken breasts, sliced into 1" strips
1 cup dahl (tiny lentils)
6 cups chicken broth
2 cups frozen vegetables (carrots, limas, corn, peas etc.)
1 can coconut milk
A few sprigs cilantro (for garnish)

Directions

In a large soup pot saute the onion, garlic, potato, carrot and spices in oil and butter until translucent. Stir in the chicken and fry until lightly browned, about 5-10 minutes. Add the dahl and fry for another few minutes. Add the chicken broth and frozen vegetables. Bring to a boil, cover and lower heat to simmer for 15 minutes or until the dahl is soft. Add the coconut milk and cook 5 minutes or so. Serve garnished with cilantro sprigs.

Prep Time	**15 minutes**
Cooking Time	**30 minutes**
Portions	**2 main courses or 4 first courses**
Taste Meter	**4½ - Tasty, fragrant and rich**
Health Meter	**2 - Fairly healthy**
Calorie Meter	**2 - Moderate**
Budget Meter	**2 - Moderate**
Ease Meter	**1½ - Not too much work**
Exotic Meter	**2½ - Very different, but not if you are into yoga**

SOTO AYAM WITH FRESHLY GROUND SPICES & RICE NOODLES (Indonesia) [v]

Soto Ayam is very popular in Indonesia. This is an adaptation from a recipe I found in the New York Times (a distant suburb of Jakarta). Not much trouble to prepare, I found it to be authentic.

Ingredients

1 cup boneless chicken meat or 2 thawed breasts, sliced
3 cans chicken broth
2 stalks lemon grass, tied and bruised
Kaffir lime leaves (optional)
1 tsp black peppercorns (or use pre-ground pepper)
1 tsp each coriander and cumin seeds (or use powdered versions)
1 tsp powdered chili (you pick the heat)
3 cloves garlic, finely chopped
2 tbsp minced ginger root
1 tbsp ground turmeric
1 tsp salt
1 oz peanut oil or butter, clarified if possible
1 can bamboo shoots
1 cup dry rice noodles
1 oz lime juice

Directions

In a soup pot simmer the chicken meat in the broth with the lemon grass and lime leaves for 30 minutes, skimming off any scum that develops. Remove the chicken, lemon grass and lime leaves. Grind the peppercorns, coriander and cumin seeds in a mortar and pestle or food processor. Add the garlic, ginger, turmeric, and salt, mixing in a little water to make a paste. Heat in peanut oil or clarified butter in a skillet a few minutes. Add the chicken and sauté for 10 minutes. Meanwhile, place the rice noodles in boiling water and simmer for 5-10 minutes until tender. Put the chicken mixture, bamboo shoots, and noodles into the soup. Add the lime juice, turn off the heat, let sit 5 minutes and serve.

Prep Time	**20 minutes**
Cooking Time	**50 minutes**
Portions	**2 main courses or 4 first courses**
Taste Meter	**3 - Very good flavor and nicely spiced**
Health Meter	**2½ - Very healthy**
Calorie Meter	**1½ - Fairly low-cal**
Budget Meter	**2 - Moderate**
Ease Meter	**2 - Moderate**
Exotic Meter	**2½ - Different, whether you do yoga or not**

AB GOSHT WITH LIMA BEANS, LEMON & TURMERIC (Iran)

This is a lovely Persian soup with a golden yellow color from its liberal use of turmeric. Cooked the old fashioned long way, it takes a while, but nevertheless is fairly easy to prepare.

Ingredients

1 whole chicken, cut into pieces
2 oz olive oil
Juice of 4 lemons
1 tbsp dried mint
3 tbsp turmeric
salt and pepper
10 cups water
1 large onion, chopped
3 cloves garlic, minced
½ cup parsley, minced
2 potatoes, cubed
1 can lima beans with liquid
1 can chickpeas with liquid
Powdered sumac for garnish

Directions

Marinate the chicken pieces with olive oil, half the lemon juice and spices for 30 minutes. Boil the water in a large soup pot. Put the chicken, onion, garlic, parsley, and potatoes in the pot. Bring to a boil, cover, and reduce the heat to simmer. Skim the foam and cook for an hour. Towards the end of the cooking time add the canned beans and more lemon juice. Serve with basmati rice and garnish with powdered sumac.

Prep Time	**15 minutes**
Cooking Time	**90 minutes**
Portions	**3-4 main courses or 4-8 first courses**
Taste Meter	**3½ - Yummy yellow turmeric broth**
Health Meter	**2 - Fairly healthy**
Calorie Meter	**2 - Moderate**
Budget Meter	**2 - Moderately cheap**
Ease Meter	**1½ - Time consuming, but fairly easy**
Exotic Meter	**2½ - Take your aunt shopping for a Persian carpet to get her ready for this**

CHICKEN SOUP WITH DUMPLINGS (Ireland)

From the Emerald Isle this easily made soup is comfort food personified, a true working class meal guaranteed to turn the luck of the shamrock your way. It is easily worth an Irish blessing or two. ("May the road rise to meet you" or "May you arrive in heaven an hour before the devil knows you're dead." Your choice.)

Ingredients
2 cans condensed cream of chicken soup
4 cups water
4 skinless, boneless chicken breast halves, sliced
1 cup chopped celery stalks and leaves
2 onions, sliced
3 potatoes, cubed
4 carrots, sliced
1 leek, sliced
1 tbsp each poultry seasoning and thyme
Salt and pepper
1 tbsp baking powder
1 cup all purpose flour
¾ cup milk
1 oz each melted butter and canola oil
1 cup frozen peas

Directions
Ina large heavy pot, combine the canned soup, water, chicken, celery, onions, potatoes, carrots, leek, herbs, salt and pepper. Bring to a boil, cover and simmer for 30 minutes. Meanwhile prepare the dumplings by mixing the milk, butter and oil into the flour and knead for a couple of minutes. Shape into spoonfuls and drop into either boiling water or the soup itself and cook for 10 minutes. Add the peas, cook 5 minutes more and serve.

Prep Time	**20 minutes**
Cooking Time	**50 minutes**
Portions	**2 main courses or 4 first courses**
Taste Meter	**4½ - As yummy as the inside of a pot pie**
Health Meter	**1½ - Hearty, but not too healthful**
Calorie Meter	**2½ - Fairly rich**
Budget Meter	**2 - Moderately inexpensive**
Ease Meter	**2 - Moderate**
Exotic Meter	**1 - As exotic as an Irish potato**

CHICKEN SOUP WITH FENNEL, ZUCCHINI & TORTELLINI (Italy) [v]

Italy is a nation where soup reigns supreme from minestrone to stracciatella. This easy recipe with tortellini and finochio (fennel) would make me moonstruck even if I hadn't watched the movie.

Ingredients

2 oz olive oil
1 onion, chopped
4 cloves garlic, minced
2 celery ribs, thinly sliced
½ green bell pepper, thinly sliced
½ cup Italian parsley, finely chopped
1 tbsp each fresh or dried oregano and basil
2 tsp fennel seeds
1 tsp dried crushed red pepper
Salt and pepper
3 cans chicken broth
1½ cups leftover chicken or thawed breast strips, cubed
½ cup fennel leaves, chopped finely
2 zucchini, diced
2 carrots, diced
1 potato, diced
1 package fresh cheese tortellini
Lemon slices
2 oz Pecorino-Romano cheese, grated

Directions

Put the olive oil in a large soup pot and saute the garlic and onions over a medium heat until soft. Add the celery, bell pepper, parsley, and spices. Cook until tender, about 10 minutes. Add the broth, bring to a boil, cover, and simmer for 10 minutes. Add the chicken, fennel, zucchini, carrots and potato, cooking another 10 minutes. Add the ravioli and cook until heated through, about 5 minutes. Serve with lemon slices and sprinkle on some grated cheese.

Prep Time	**15 minutes**
Cooking Time	**40 minutes**
Portions	**2 main courses or 4 first courses**
Taste Meter	**4½ - This is so good!**
Health Meter	**2 - Fairly healthy**
Calorie Meter	**2 - Moderate**
Budget Meter	**2 – Moderate**
Ease Meter	**1½ - Fairly easy**
Exotic Meter	**1½ - Outside of the fennel, nothing unusual**

CHICKEN SOUP WITH DASHI, SHIITAKE MUSHROOMS, TOFU & NAPA CABBAGE (Japan)

Japanese soups are usually started with dashi, which is a mixture of dried fish flakes and seaweed. I found a tasty recipe in an old cookbook of mine, which I adapted to this traditional base.

Ingredients

1 kombo (seaweed) square
½ cup dried bonito flakes
3 cups water
2 cans chicken broth
2 oz soy sauce
1 oz Mirin or rice wine
1 tbsp sesame oil
1 cup leftover boneless chicken or thawed breast strips, cubed
3 tbsp ginger root, minced
3 shiiitake mushrooms, soaked, softened and sliced
1 tsp red chili flakes
1 cup udon or rice noodles
1 cup tofu, cut into small cubes
6 small scallions, chopped fine
2 cups sliced Napa cabbage

Directions

Place the seaweed square in a saucepan of water along with the fish flakes. Bring to a boil and the turn off the heat. Add some soy sauce and let this steep for a couple of minutes, Strain the ingredients and transfer the broth to a soup pot. Add the chicken broth, soy sauce, sesame oil, chicken, ginger root, chili flakes and mushroom slices, simmering for about 5 minutes. Add the udon, tofu, scallions and Napa cabbage and continue simmering another 5 minutes. Serve immediately.

Prep Time	**15 minutes**
Cooking Time	**20 minutes**
Portions	**2 main courses or 4 first courses**
Taste Meter	**3½ - Quite tasty**
Health Meter	**3 - Very healthy**
Calorie Meter	**1½ - Fairly slimming**
Budget Meter	**1½ - Fairly inexpensive**
Ease Meter	**1½ - Fairly easy to make**
Exotic Meter	**2½ - Definitely different, you may need to give your aunt a cup of sake first**

CHICKEN SOUP WITH EGGPLANT, OKRA & PEANUT BUTTER (Kenya) [v]

My browser took me on a culinary safari to find this delightful soup from the other side of the world. Smooth or chunky, it's the peanuttiest. Obama's African side of the family would like this one.

Ingredients

½ onion, chopped
3 cloves garlic, diced
1 cup diced eggplant
1 oz olive oil
1 tbsp curry powder
1 tsp powdered chili
2 tbsp tomato paste (or 1 can tomato sauce)
1 cup chicken leftovers or thawed frozen breasts, sliced
5 cups chicken broth
1 cup peanut butter
1 can diced tomatoes
1 butternut, zucchini or other squash, diced
1 cup frozen okra
1 large potato, diced
1 oz. lime juice
Salt & pepper

Directions

In a frying pan saute the onions, garlic and eggplant in olive oil. Add curry and chili powders and tomato paste. Add the chicken meat and sauté until the chicken is cooked. Put aside to let flavors mingle. Put the chicken broth in a soup pot and bring to a boil, then reduce to simmer. Add the tomatoes, peanut butter, potato, and squash. Stir well. Bring to another boil and then lower to simmer. Add the chicken mixture, lime juice, salt and pepper and cook for another 20 minutes.

Prep Time	**15 minutes**
Cooking Time	**30 minutes**
Portions	**2 main courses or 4 first courses**
Taste Meter	**4 - A souper adventure**
Health Meter	**2 - Moderately healthy**
Calorie Meter	**1½ - Fairly low-cal**
Budget Meter	**1½ - Reasonably cheap**
Ease Meter	**1½ - Fairly easy to make**
Exotic Meter	**2½ - Not found in Campbell's or Progresso**

SAM GYE TANG WITH GINSENG ROOT AND RED DATES (Korea)

This Korean soup is an adaptation of an adaptation from a restaurant in Seoul. Finding the herbs may take some searching. It mixes subtle bitter, sweet and savory flavors. Red pepper flakes can give the dish added heat. The ginseng is reputed to have strong healing properties as well as promoting energy. After consuming this soup, I could feel myself sweating out toxins.

Ingredients

2 thawed Cornish game hens
½ cup sweet rice
4 pieces dried ginseng root
2 cloves garlic, cubed
1 oz ginger root, cubed
8 red dates (jujubes)
8 cups water
2 green onions
1 cup Napa cabbage, sliced
1 cup bean sprouts
Korean hot red pepper flakes (to taste)
Salt and pepper

Directions

Wash the rice and set aside. Thaw the Cornish game hens and rinse them well before cooking. Stuff the hens with a mixture of rice, ginseng, garlic, ginger root, and red dates. The rice will expand during cooking. Tie up the hens if possible or fill snugly to keep the ingredients inside. Place in a large soup pot and bring to a boil, skimming off any scum that forms. Cover and simmer for an hour. Add the cabbage, green onions, bean sprouts and chili flakes and cook for 5 more minutes. Turn off the heat. Serve with marinated vegetables, kim chee (bottled Napa cabbage in chili and anchovy pastes) and a bowl of sticky rice on the side.

Prep Time	30 minutes
Cooking Time	60 minutes
Portions	2 main courses or 4-6 first courses
Taste Meter	3 - Subtle taste until the chili and kim chee take over
Health Meter	3+ - Incredibly healthful
Calorie Meter	1 - Very slimming
Budget Meter	3 - Very pricy
Ease Meter	2 - Some cooking skills needed
Exotic Meter	3 - So different, your aunt may need a whole carafe of sake

CHICKEN SORREL SOUP (Latvia) [v]

This recipe was an offhand request from one of my friends thinking I'd never find one from her homeland. However, one search on the internet and I met her challenge. Another friend just so happens to raise sorrel in her garden. How serendipitous! This light dish is more suitable for a first course than a square meal.

Ingredients

1 cup boneless chicken leftovers or thawed breast, sliced
1 onion, chopped
1 oz butter
1 quart chicken broth
2 carrots, diced
2 potatoes, diced
½ cup green onions, chopped
1 tbsp fresh dill, chopped
1 tbsp chives, chopped
Salt & pepper
1 cup sorrel leaves, shredded (spinach can be substituted)
2 medium hard-boiled eggs, chopped (for garnish)
Sour cream to taste

Directions

In a soup pot saute the chicken and onion in butter. Add the broth, carrots, potatoes, green onions, herbs and salt and pepper. Bring to a boil, lower the heat, and simmer for 20 minutes. Add the sorrel leaves (or spinach) and cook another 10 minutes. Serve garnished with the hard-boiled egg and a dollop of sour cream.

Prep Time	**15 minutes**
Cooking Time	**30 minutes**
Portions	**2 main courses or 4 first courses**
Taste Meter	**2½ - Gentle lemony flavor from the sorrel**
Health Meter	**2 - Fairly healthy**
Calorie Meter	**2 - Depends on how much sour cream**
Budget Meter	**1½ - Fairly cheap**
Ease Meter	**1½ - Very easy to make**
Exotic Meter	**1½ - As exotic as sour cream**

CHICKEN SOUP WITH RED LENTILS, CUMIN, & CILANTRO (Lebanon) [v]

A hearty easy-to-prepare inexpensive first course or light meal. This dish has just enough spice without being overpowering.

Ingredients

6 cups chicken stock
2 cups red lentils
1 cup cubed leftover or thawed chicken meat
1 onion, chopped
3 cloves garlic, diced
3 tbsp olive oil
1 tsp cayenne pepper
1 tbsp cumin
Salt & pepper
½ cup lemon juice
½ cup chopped cilantro

Directions

Bring the stock to a boil in a soup pan, lower the heat and stir in the lentils. Cover and simmer for 15 minutes. Add the chicken meat and cook another 10 minutes. Meanwhile, saute the onion and garlic in the olive oil in a frying pan until translucent, about 3 minutes Stir in the spices. Add to the broth and cook another 5 minutes. Add the lemon juice and cilantro and cook a few minutes more. Serve immediately.

Prep Time	**15 minutes**
Cooking Time	**30 minutes**
Portions	**2 main courses or 4-6 first courses**
Taste Meter	**4 - Excellent**
Health Meter	**3 - Very healthy**
Calorie Meter	**1½ - Fairly slimming**
Budget Meter	**1½ - Fairly cheap**
Ease Meter	**1 - Easy to make this one**
Exotic Meter	**2 - Different, but hardly a threat**

CALDO DE BOLITAS DE TORTILLA
(Mexico) [v]

South of the U.S. border there is a rich tradition of caldos and sopas. Growing up in Los Angeles, I have enjoyed many of them in our vast array of Mexican restaurants. Here is an adaptation of an unusual recipe I found in an old Mexican cookbook.

Ingredients

12 tortillas (stale is OK)
1 cup milk
1 onion, finely chopped
2 cloves garlic, minced
¼ cup grated Parmesan cheese
½ cup flour
Several sprigs of epazote (if available) or parsley
2 eggs, beaten
4 cans chicken broth
1 zucchini, sliced
1 can diced tomatoes (with liquid)
2 ears fresh corn on the cob, quartered
1 cup cubed chicken meat
2 serrano chilis, seeded and minced
1 tbsp oregano
2 oz lemon juice
Salt & pepper
A few sprigs cilantro (for garnish)

Directions

Soak the tortillas in milk. When soft, place them and the leftover milk in an electric bender with the garlic and onion and blend until smooth. Combine with the cheese, flour, epazote, eggs, salt and pepper. Chill in the refrigerator. Meanwhile, heat the chicken broth in a soup pot, adding the zucchini, tomatoes, corn, chicken, oregano and lemon juice. Bring to a boil, cover, and simmer for 15 minutes. Take the tortilla mixture and form into small balls, dropping into the boiling water for 10 minutes. Transfer to the soup.

Prep Time	25 minutes
Cooking Time	30 minutes
Portions	2-3 main courses or 4-6 first courses
Taste Meter	5 - Amazing flavor in both soup and bolitas
Health Meter	2 - Moderate
Calorie Meter	2 - Moderate
Budget Meter	2 - Moderately inexpensive
Ease Meter	2½ - A fair amount of work
Exotic Meter	2 - My mother would have loved these Mexican matzo balls

HUNSEKJUTTSUPPE WITH APPLES & VEGETABLES (Norway) [v]

This recipe is an easy-to-prepare light meal that balances sweet and savory flavors. Who knew that apples and leeks would make such good soupfellows.

Ingredients

3 tbsp butter
1 leek, white portion only, cleaned and thinly sliced
1 carrot, diced
1 parsnip, diced
3 tbsp flour
4 cups broth
2 medium Granny Smith or other tart apple, peeled and sliced
1½ cups cooked diced cooked chicken meat
Salt & pepper

Directions

Melt butter in a soup pan and slowly sauté the leek, carrot, and parsnip for a few minutes until they soften but do not brown. Stir in the flour and cook for 5 minutes, stirring until well blended. Add the broth, stirring vigorously. Simmer gently for 10 minutes or until the soup is smooth and slightly thick. Add the apple slices and chicken meat. Simmer 10 minutes longer. Season and serve.

Prep Time	**15 minutes**
Cooking Time	**30 minutes**
Portions	**2 main courses or 4 first courses**
Taste Meter	**4½ - Surprisingly fabulous**
Health Meter	**2½ - Fairly healthful**
Calorie Meter	**2 - Moderate**
Budget Meter	**2 - Moderately cheap**
Ease Meter	**2 - Fairy easy to make**
Exotic Meter	**2 - Different in a subtle way**

CHICKEN SOUP WITH POTATOES & CILANTRO SALSA (Peru) [v]

A fairly light exotically spiced first course or supper dish. I've been served this wonderful cilantro salsa in some L.A. Peruvian restaurants and it is so worth the extra work. I'll green up my soup bowl with this sauce anytime.

Ingredients

2 skinless boneless chicken breasts
2 oz olive oil
2 oz lemon juice
1 medium onion, chopped
3 cloves garlic, diced
½ green or red bell pepper
2 serrano chilis, seeded and minced
6 cups chicken broth
1 cup green peas
1 cup fresh or frozen corn
2 oz finely chopped cilantro
3 potatoes, sliced
1 cup uncooked rice
Salt & pepper

Directions

Marinate the chicken meat in half the olive oil and lemon juice, and salt and pepper. Heat the remaining olive oil in a large pot and stir in the onion, garlic, serrano chili and cook until soft, about 2 minutes. Add the chicken and cook 5 minutes longer. Stir in the cilantro, corn, peas, and bell pepper and cook another 5 minutes. Pour in the chicken broth, cut-up potatoes, remaining lemon juice and rice. Simmer until the potatoes are tender, about 20-30 minutes. Serve with cilantro salsa.

Prep Time	**20 minutes**
Cooking Time	**40 minutes**
Portions	**2 main courses or 4 first courses**
Taste Meter	**4½ - A real pleasure**
Health Meter	**2½ - Very healthy**
Calorie Meter	**1½ - Fairly low in calories**
Budget Meter	**2 - Moderately cheap**
Ease Meter	**1½ - Fairly easy to make**
Exotic Meter	**1½ - Fairly straightforward**

CILANTRO SALSA

Ingredients

1 large bunch of fresh cilantro leaves
3 oz olive oil
2 oz lime juice
2 cloves garlic
1 sliced hot green pepper (serrano or jalapeno)
Salt & pepper

Directions

Wash and chop the cilantro leaves and put in a blender or food processor. Add the rest of the ingredients and blend or pulse slightly, just enough to make the salsa smooth, but not over-processed. Taste and adjust seasonings as necessary.

Prep Time	**5 minutes**
Cooking Time	**0**
Portions	**Enough for several meals**
Taste Meter	**5 - A true culinary pleasure**
Health Meter	**3 - Very healthy**
Calorie Meter	**1½ - Fairly low in calories**
Budget Meter	**1½ - Moderately cheap**
Ease Meter	**1½ - Fairly easy to make**
Exotic Meter	**2½ - It's got a bit of a bite**

CALDO VERDE WITH KALE, LINGUICA & WHITE BEANS (Portugal) [v]

Many consider this hearty soup to be the national dish of Portugal. It is not difficult to make, yet impressive enough to serve guests. A glass of Portuguese rose would only embellish this great dish.

Ingredients

1 oz olive oil
2 linguica sausages, sliced
1 onion, chopped
3 cloves garlic, diced
3 cans broth
4 large potatoes, sliced
1 can navy or cannellini beans
1 lb kale, coarse stems and veins removed, chopped thinly.
Salt & pepper

Directions

In a large soup pan, saute the sausages, onion and garlic in olive oil about 5 minutes. Add the broth and potatoes, bring to boil, then cover and simmer for 15 additional minutes. Put the canned beans and chopped kale into the soup pot and cook 5-10 minutes more.

Prep Time	**15 minutes**
Cooking Time	**30 minutes**
Portions	**2 main courses or 4 first courses**
Taste Meter	**4 - Worth repeating**
Health Meter	**2 - Fairly healthy**
Calorie Meter	**2 - Moderate**
Budget Meter	**2 - Moderately cheap**
Ease Meter	**1½ - Fairly easy to make**
Exotic Meter	**2 - Right down the middle of different**

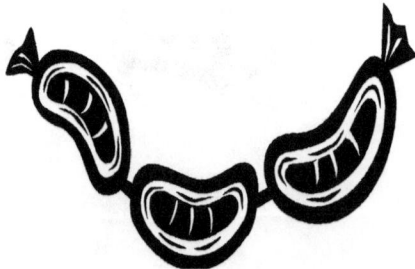

ASOPOA WITH RECAITO AND PLANTAIN DUMPLINGS (Puerto Rico)

This is a rich tropical soup, perfect for a balmy night. Too much work for a throw together meal, but worth the effort for a weekend or make-ahead dish. A rum drink would be a suitable accompaniment.

Ingredients
2 cups chicken, cut into serving pieces
1 tbsp adobo or chili powder
1 oz lime juice
2 oz olive oil
4 oz smoked ham, diced
3 tbsp annatto oil if available (or chili oil)
1 onion, chopped
3 cloves garlic, diced
4 oz recaito (see below)
1 8-oz can tomato sauce
16 cups water
1 cup uncooked rice
Salt and pepper
1 package frozen peas
1 small can pimentos (for garnish)

Directions
Rub the chicken pieces with adobo or chili powder and lime juice and half the oil. Let sit. Meanwhile, in a large soup pot saute the ham, garlic and onions in the remaining oil for a few minutes. Add the recaito and tomato sauce and cook a little longer. Add the water, chicken, rice, salt and pepper. Bring to a boil, skimming the foam off the top. Cover, lower the heat and simmer for 40 minutes. Meanwhile, prepare the plantain dumplings and spoon them into the soup for another 15 minutes of cooking time. Add the peas and pimentos, and cook 5 minutes longer.

RECAITO
Ingredients
½ small green pepper
½ medium onion
2 cloves garlic
¼ cup cilantro leaves
Salt and pepper

Directions
Chop the ingredients very fine or better yet combine in a food processor or blender.

PLANTAIN DUMPLINGS
Ingredients
1 large green plantain, peeled and shredded
Salt and pepper
Directions
Grate the plantain finely side of a grater. Add salt and pepper and form into small balls. These simple dumplings take a bit of practice to get right. Cook in the chicken broth for 15 minutes.

Prep Time	**20-10-10 minutes**
Cooking Time	**60-10-20 minutes**
Portions	**2-4 main courses or 6-8 first courses**
Taste Meter	**4 - soup, 4 - recaito, 2½ - dumplings**
Health Meter	**2 - Fairly healthy**
Calorie Meter	**2 - Not too fattening**
Budget Meter	**2 - Moderate**
Ease Meter	**1½ - A fair amount of work**
Exotic Meter	**3 - Decidedly different**

*"Is that a plantain in your pocket
or are you just glad to see me?"*

Mae West to her Don Juan in San Juan

CHICKEN SOUP WITH OGOURZI (Russia) [v]

This recipe is a very unique soup with its celery root flavor and sour cream finish. Only use the tender insides of the celery root as the outsides can be a bit tough. Who knew that croutons from rye bread existed under the Tzars in the motherland? Your Russian mother knows. A little more sour cream, please.

Ingredients

½ onion, chopped
3 cloves garlic, diced
1 oz oil
1 quart chicken broth
1 large potato, diced
2 cups diced celeriac (celery root)
1 tbsp fresh or dried dill to taste
1 tbsp dry mustard
Salt & pepper to taste
1 cup asparagus, sliced
1 cup cabbage, sliced
1 egg, beaten
Ogourzi (rye bread croutons)
½ cup sour cream

Directions

In a soup pot saute the garlic and onions in oil. Add the chicken broth, potato, celery root and spices. Bring to a boil, then simmer for 15 minutes. Add the asparagus and cabbage and cook another 15 minutes. Beat the egg in a bowl, adding a small amount of broth to temper. Serve with ogourzi and sour cream.

Prep Time	**15 minutes**
Cooking Time	**40 minutes**
Portions	**2 main courses or 4 first courses**
Taste Meter	**3½ - Dill and sour cream work well**
Health Meter	**2 - Moderately healthy**
Calorie Meter	**2 – Depends on how much sour cram**
Budget Meter	**2 - Moderate**
Ease Meter	**1½ - Fairly easy to make**
Exotic meter	**1½ - Middle of the Russian road**

OGOURZI (RYE BREAD CROUTONS)

Ingredients

6 slices rye bread
2 tbsp butter
2 tbsp oil
1 clove garlic, chopped
1 tbsp fresh or dried dill weed

Directions

Cut crusts from the rye bread and dice into ½-in cubes. Saute with the chopped garlic and dill weed in butter and oil until well coated. Bake in a 300-degree oven until crisp (20 to 30 minutes). Serve with the soup.

Prep Time -	**15 minutes**
Cooking Time	**30 minutes**
Portions	**2 main courses or 4 first courses**
Taste Meter	**4 - A truly unique taste sensation**
Health Meter	**1½ - Not particularly healthy**
Calorie Meter	**2½ - Fairly rich**
Budget Meter	**2 - Moderate**
Ease Meter	**1½ - Not hard to make**
Exotic Meter	**2 - Different but not too**

"Mankind can't live by bread alone,
but chicken soup may be another matter."

COCK-A-LEEKIE SOUP (Scotland)

This is a traditional soup made with prunes that dates back to the sixteenth century. It is a popular winter dish often served at Burns Suppers or on St. Andrew's Night (November 30th).

Ingredients

1 whole chicken, cut up or several leftover or thawed chicken pieces
3 slices bacon, cut into pieces
8 cups water
1-2 lbs leeks (6-12)
1 large potato, cubed
½ cup chopped parsley
1 tsp fresh or dried thyme
1 bay leaf
Salt and pepper
½ cup uncooked rice
4 oz cooked prunes with pits removed
1 tsp brown sugar

Directions

Place the chicken pieces and bacon in a large soup pan and cover with the water. Bring to a boil and remove any scum that forms. Add half the leeks, potato, the herbs, salt and pepper, cover and simmer for an hour. Remove the chicken pieces and shred. Add the chicken, rice, remaining leeks, prunes and sugar. Cook another 30 minutes. Serve with haggis and later with shortbread for dessert.

Prep Time	**15 minutes**
Cooking Time	**100 minutes**
Portions	**2-4 main courses or 4-8 first courses**
Taste Meter	**3 - Interesting variation with the prunes**
Health Meter	**2 - Fairly healthy**
Calorie Meter	**2 - Moderate**
Budget Meter	**2 - Moderately cheap**
Ease Meter	**2½ - Fairly easy to make**
Exotic Meter	**1½ - If you find bacon and prunes exotic, so be it**

SOPA DE POLLO CON PIMENTOS Y FIDEOS (Spain) [v]

This first course is very popular throughout Spain. It is also a good light supper item. A crusty loaf of bread and some Rioja region wine would make a well-fitting accompaniment.

Ingredients

3 celery sticks, chopped
2 carrots, chopped
½ each onion and bell pepper, chopped
3 cloves garlic, diced
3 tbsp olive oil
2 chicken backs (or whatever parts you wish)
6 cups water
1 tbsp paprika
2 bay leaves
1 8 oz can pimentos
Pinch of saffron
Salt and pepper
¼ lb angel hair pasta

Directions

Peel and coarsely chop the vegetables. Put the olive oil in a large soup pot and saute the vegetables for a few minutes, stirring constantly. Add the chicken backs and brown for 2-3 minutes more. Add the water, paprika and bay leaves. Simmer for an hour or so, skimming the scum off the top of the broth. The chicken should be soft and ready to fall off the bones. Remove the backs, cool and de-bone them. Also take out the bay leaves. Break the pasta in half. Add the pimentos, saffron and pasta and return the chicken meat to the broth. Cook a few minutes longer and serve.

Prep Time	**15 minutes**
Cooking Time	**90 minutes**
Portions	**2 main courses or 4 first courses**
Taste Meter	**4½ - Subtle, but excellent flavor**
Health Meter	**2½ - Very healthy**
Calorie Meter	**1½ - Fairly low-cal**
Budget Meter	**1½ - Fairly cheap**
Ease Meter	**1½ - Very easy to make**
Exotic Meter	**1½ - Familiar as long as your aunt likes pimentos**

CHICKEN SOUP WITH CARDAMOM-ALMOND DUMPLINGS (Sweden) [v]

Good for a light one-course dinner or supper, this hearty soup hails from a northern clime where dairy products rule. The dumplings are different than most and flavored with a Swedish favorite, cardamom.

Ingredients

6 cups chicken stock
2 cups cooked chicken meat
1 cup celery stalks and leaves, sliced
1 onion, chopped
3 cloves garlic, minced
1 potato, cubed
3 stalks celery, chopped
1 tbsp dried thyme
salt and pepper
1 cup frozen peas

DUMPLINGS

4 oz flour
2 oz butter
1½ cups milk
4 cardamom seeds, crushed or 1 tbsp powdered cardamom
1 egg
16 almonds, run in a food processor or blender or chop very finely
2 tbsp parsley, minced
Salt & pepper

Directions

Heat the chicken stock, chicken, celery, onion, garlic and spices in a soup pot. Bring to boil, then cover and simmer for 30 minutes. Meanwhile, in a separate saucepan blend the flour and butter over a low heat and gradually add the milk, stirring constantly until thickened. Beat the egg, warm with a little broth, add to the flour mixture, knead slightly and cool. Add the almonds and parsley, form into balls and drop in the boiling soup. Season with salt and pepper, add the frozen peas and cook for a few minutes until the dumplings rise to the top. Serve immediately.

Prep Time	**20 minutes**
Cooking Time	**50 minutes**
Portions	**2 main courses or 4 first courses**
Taste Meter	**3 - soup, 5 - dumplings**
Health Meter	**2 - Moderately healthy**
Calorie Meter	**2½ - Fairly rich**
Budget Meter	**2 - Fairly inexpensive**
Ease Meter	**2½ - A little work, but so worth it**
Exotic Meter	**2 - The dumplings are out of this world!**

TOM KHA GAI WITH LEMON GRASS, GALANGAL & COCONUT MILK (Thailand)

It takes more time to find the ingredients than to prepare this soup. This dish is easy to make, yet complex in flavor, and the coconut milk makes it a real treat. This soup is often served in over-the-flame containers in Thai restaurants as a first course, but also works on top of rice for a main course. To make this dish more substantial, add some canned Asian vegetables such as bamboo shoots.

Ingredients

2 cans chicken broth
2 or more pieces of lemon grass, bruised to release flavor
2 large cubes of galangal root (or ginger root if not available)
4 kaffir lime leaves (if available)
2 thawed boneless chicken breasts, cubed
2 oz fish sauce
1 oz lime juice
1 can coconut milk
1 tbsp brown sugar
½ can straw mushrooms
1 can baby corn
Several small thai or serrano chilis, sliced finely, keeping the seeds
A few sprigs cilantro (for garnish)

Directions

Heat the chicken stock and add the lemon grass, lime leaves and galangal or ginger root. Bring to a boil, then turn heat down to simmer. Add the chicken breasts, fish sauce, mushrooms, baby corn, lime juice, sugar and coconut milk. Keep simmering for a few minutes until the chicken is fully cooked. When you serve this soup you may want to remove the lemon grass, galangal, lime leaves, and chilis. Eating these chilis is advisable only if a fire extinguisher is present. Cilantro leaves make a nice garnish.

Prep Time	**10 minutes**
Cooking Time	**20 minutes**
Portions	**2 main courses or 4 first courses**
Taste Meter	**5 - State of the art!**
Health Meter	**2½ - Fairly healthy**
Calorie Meter	**2 - Moderately rich**
Budget Meter	**2 - Moderate**
Ease Meter	**1½ - Fairly easy to make**
Exotic Meter	**2½ - Years ago this would have been off the charts, but with today's Thai food popularity, who knows?**

CHORBA WITH COUSCOUS (Tunisia) [v]

A popular soup in this North African country, this dish is exotic, spicy and comforting. My house smelled so fragrant afterwards, I was ready to rent a camel and ride out to get more ingredients for the following day. Accompanying this dish with peppermint tea could help to balance its strong flavors.

Ingredients

1 onion, chopped
3 cloves garlic, diced
1 tomato, chopped
2 carrots, diced
½ cup parsley, chopped
2 oz. olive oil
1 tbsp each turmeric and paprika
1 tsp each ground cumin and cinnamon
1-2 cups chicken meat leftovers or thawed breasts, cubed
4-6 cups chicken broth
1 can tomato sauce
2 oz lemon juice
Salt & pepper
A few sprigs cilantro (for garnish)
1 cup packaged couscous (optional)
1½ cups boiling water (optional)

Directions

Saute the onions, garlic and chopped vegetables in olive oil in a large soup pan. Add the spices and chicken meat, stirring for 5 minutes. Let sit a few minutes for the flavors to settle. Add the chicken broth, tomato sauce, lemon juice, and salt and pepper. Bring to a boil and reduce to simmer. Cook another 10-15 minutes. Serve garnished with cilantro. The preceding is for traditional chorba. I took the liberty of putting some couscous in a small pot of boiling water, turning off the heat, and covering for a few minutes. Adding this to the soup gave it more texture and made it more filing.   One can also serve a clear bowl of soup with couscous on the side.

Prep Time	**25 minutes**
Cooking Time	**30 minutes**
Portions	**2 main courses or 4-6 first courses**
Taste Meter	**4 - Quite sensual**
Health Meter	**2½ - Very healthy**
Calorie Meter	**1½ - Fairly low-cal**
Budget Meter	**1½ - Fairly cheap**
Ease Meter	**2 - Moderately easy to make**
Exotic Meter	**2½ - Show your aunt a DVD of Casablanca**

EZOGELIN WITH BULGUR & RED LENTILS (Turkey) [v]

This is a popular wedding soup, excellent for a supper or a light meal. "Ezo gelin corbasi" is Turkish for "the soup of Ezo the bride". I found a website with photos of an easy step-by-step process of how to make this. It's a very successful marriage of ingredients.

Ingredients

2 tbsp olive oil
2tbsp butter
1 large onion, chopped
6 cloves garlic, chopped
1 large tomato or 1 can tomato sauce
2 oz tomato paste
1 tbsp each paprika and cayenne pepper
Salt & pepper
½ cup bulgur
1 cup red lentils
¼ cup white rice
4-6 cups chicken broth
2 tbsp fresh or dried mint, chopped
2 tbsp lemon juice

Directions

Saute the onion and garlic in the olive oil and butter in a soup pot for a few minutes. Add the tomato, tomato paste and spices and cook a few minutes more. Add the grains and broth, bring to a boil, cover and simmer for 15 minutes. Stir in the lemon juice and mint. Cook for a few more minutes and serve immediately.

Prep Time	**15 minutes**
Cooking Time	**30 minutes**
Portions	**2 main courses or 4-6 first courses**
Taste Meter	**4 - Worth serving at any wedding**
Health Meter	**3 - Very healthy**
Calorie Meter	**1 - Very slimming**
Budget Meter	**1½ - Fairly inexpensive**
Ease Meter	**1½ - Fairly easy to make**
Exotic Meter	**2 - Weddings tend to be familiar, not strange**

CHICKEN SOUP WITH CABBAGE, PICKLES, ASPARAGUS & PEROGI (Ukraine)

This recipe is time consuming, but well worth the effort when you have the inclination. It is a soup festive enough for a holiday meal and can be can be made with or without the perogi. I feel that as long as one is going to take on its challenge, go all out.

Ingredients

8 cups water
1 lb or more cut up fresh, thawed or leftover chicken parts
1 onion, chopped
2 cloves garlic, diced
2 celery ribs, sliced
2 carrots, sliced
½ cup parsley root, chopped (or parsley leaves)
1 large bay leaf
1 tbsp each paprika and dried dill
Several fresh thyme sprigs (or 1 tbsp dried)
Salt & pepper
1 tbsp butter
2 cups chopped green cabbage
I cup fresh asparagus, sliced
4 oz garlic dill pickles, diced (plus 1 oz juice if desired)
2 oz tomato paste or 1 small can tomato sauce
Sour cream for garnish

Directions

Put the chicken meat, onion, vegetables and spices in boiling water, then simmer for an hour. Remove the chicken, debone if needed and cut into small pieces. Meanwhile, melt the butter in a frying pan and add the cabbage, onion, asparagus and pickles and cook over medium heat for 10 minutes. Stir in the tomato paste or sauce and cook a couple of minutes more. Add this mixture to the chicken broth as well as the chicken meat. Simmer for an additional 5 minutes, remove from the heat and let the flavors mellow. Serve with sour cream and perogi, if desired.

Prep Time	**30 minutes**
Cooking Time	**90 minutes**
Portions	**2 main courses or 4-6 first courses**
Taste Meter	**3 – Very good, but not a standout**
Health Meter	**2 - Moderately healthy**
Calorie Meter	**2 - Depends on the garnish**
Budget Meter	**2 - Moderate**
Ease Meter	**2 - Moderate cooking skills needed**
Exotic Meter	**2 – Slightly different**

PEROGI

Ingredients

2 cups all purpose flour
2 eggs, beaten
½ cup sour cream
½ cup water
1 tsp baking powder
2 medium potatoes, peeled and diced
4 cups boiling water
1oz butter or vegetable oil (or chicken fat for full flavor)
1 cup shredded cabbage
½ onion, chopped
1 oz butter
1 oz Parmesan cheese

Directions

In a large bowl combine the flour, baking powder, eggs, sour cream and water, stirring until you form a stiff dough. Turn onto a well-floured surface and knead gently with your fingertips until slightly sticky. Do not overwork this. Put in the refrigerator while you make the potato filling. Place the potatoes in the boiling water and simmer for 15 to 20 minutes. Meanwhile, sauté the onions, garlic and cabbage in a frying pan until soft around the edges. This should take about 10 minutes. Lower the heat and cook another 5 minutes. Set aside to cool. Drain the potatoes and mash them with a little butter and the parmesan cheese. Combine with the cabbage mixture.

Gather the dough in a ball, roll out in a sheet, cut up into squares, and fill with potato mixture. Drop the perogis in a quart of boiling water in batches, stirring occasionally. When they float to the top, cook for a couple of minutes more and remove from the water. Put into the soup and serve. Leftovers can be pan fried and served separately. With sour cream, they are a real treat.

Prep Time	**60 minutes**
Cooking Time	**30 minutes**
Portions	**2 main courses or 4-6 first courses**
Taste Meter	**3 - A bit bland, but not at all boring**
Health Meter	**3 - Quite fattening**
Calorie Meter	**2½ - Fairly rich**
Budget Meter	**1½ - Fairly cheap**
Ease Meter	**3 - A lot of cooking skills needed**
Exotic Meter	**1½ - Different, but not that strange**

CHICKEN PHO WITH CELLOPHANE RICE NOODLES & BEAN SPROUTS (Vietnam)

Delicately balanced, the art of pho takes some practice. This soup is so Vietnamese many restaurants use the word pho in their name.

Ingredients

2-4 oz thin cellophane rice noodles
1 tbsp peanut or sesame oil
8 oz boneless skinless chicken breasts, cubed
½ onion, chopped
1 tbsp garlic, minced garlic
2 tbsp minced ginger root
1 tsp red pepper flakes or powder (optional)
2 cans chicken broth
1 tbsp soy sauce
2 tbsp fish sauce
4-6 frozen shrimp (optional)
1 cup fresh bean sprouts
2 tbsp cilantro, chopped
2 tbsp green onions, chopped
¼ cup fresh Thai basil, chopped
1 tsp lime juice
Siracha chili sauce

Directions

Soak the noodles in very hot tap water. While noodles are soaking, cut chicken into strips. Heat oil in a soup pan over medium-high heat. Add the chicken, garlic, ginger and red pepper. Cook for 1 minute, then add broth, soy sauce and fish sauce, and bring to a boil. Reduce heat to simmer until chicken is done, about 5 minutes. Add shrimp and cook 5 minutes longer. Add bean sprouts, lime juice, cilantro, green onions and Thai basil, then turn off the heat. Drain noodles and cut into short pieces about 1½ inches long. Put the noodles into the soup and season with siracha sauce to taste.

Prep Time	**10 minutes**
Cooking Time	**15 minutes**
Portions	**2 main courses or 4 first courses**
Taste Meter	**4 - Not overpowering, but quite tasty**
Health Meter	**3 - Very healthy**
Calorie Meter	**3 - Slimming**
Budget Meter	**2 - Moderately cheap**
Ease Meter	**1½ - Very easy to make**
Exotic Meter	**2½ - Keep the tripe and offals out and you avoid a "3" rating**

CHICKEN SOUP WITH PUMPKIN & GOUDA CHEESE (West Indies) [v]

From a tropical soul kitchen to a temperate tummy, this recipe is a cheap vacation to the islands. Much more exotic than your mother's chicken soup, let alone your aunt's.

Ingredients

1 cup or more chicken meat leftovers or thawed breasts, sliced
1 onion, chopped
2 cloves garlic, diced
1 oz olive oil
4 cups broth
2 cups pumpkin, diced
1 can kidney beans
1 tsp powdered chili
1 tsp ground coriander
1 tsp ground caraway seeds
1 oz lime juice
1 cup gouda cheese, grated
Salt & pepper
A few sprigs cilantro (for garnish)

Directions

Saute the chicken meat in olive oil in a soup pan with the garlic and onions. Stir for a few minutes until the chicken is cooked. Add the chicken broth, kidney beans, pumpkin, lime juice and spices. Bring to a boil, reduce heat and simmer for 10 minutes. Mix in the green onions and cook another 5 to 10 minutes. Add the grated cheese. Serve garnished with cilantro.

Prep Time	**15 minutes**
Cooking Time	**30 minutes**
Portions	**2 main courses or 4 first courses**
Taste Meter	**3 - Tasty, but not a sensation**
Health Meter	**2 - Fairly healthy**
Calorie Meter	**2 - Somewhat rich**
Budget Meter	**2½ - Not cheap**
Ease Meter	**2 - Moderately easy to make**
Exotic Meter	**2- Exotic, but not to "Aunt Tillies"**

SUGGESTIONS FOR FURTHER READING

Let's Cook It Right. Adelle Davis, Harcourt, Brace & World Inc., New York

The Complete Book of Mexican Cooking. Elisabeth Lambert Ortiz, Bantam Cookbooks

Authentic Cajun Cooking. Chef Paul Prudhomme, McIlhenny Company, Avery Island, LA

The Art Of Basque Cooking. Clara Salaverria Perkins, Haskell Berry Printing & Lithograph Inc., Sacramento

A Book Of Middle Eastern Food. Claudia Roden, Vintage Books

Adventures In Indian Cooking. Mary Atwood, Jaico Publishing House, Mumbai

Joyce Chen Cookbook. Joyce Chen, J.B. Lippincott Co, Philadelphia

The Pleasures of Japanese Cooking. Heihachi Tanaka, Cornerstone Library, New York

Music For An Italian Dinner At Home. Italian String Orchestra, RCA Records (great recipes on the back of the album) [out of print]

Bon Appetit!

INDEX - CHICKEN SOUP WITH ....

ABOUT THE AUTHOR

[David] CAT COHEN has been around the block, many blocks. If you live in L.A., when Cat resided there he probably went around your block. As a traveling music teacher, co-author and chief research person for the successful cheap restaurant guidebook **DIVING OUT IN LA**, massage therapist, flower delivery person, and all-around curious guy, Cat scouted the city for ideas for his songs, musicals, poetry, books, and cookbooks. Now relocated in the high desert north of Palm Springs, he's exploring his new region's nooks and crannies as well.

A lifelong gourmet cook, Cat has shopped in so many ethnic LA markets he could qualify for a Guinness Book of Records nomination. He's traveled through 48 of our 50 states and many countries as well, sampling the native cuisines and picking up cooking tips. When he visited New Orleans, he once was Paul Prudhome's assistant in a live cooking show there.

An ASCAP and NARAS songwriter, Cat has had songs recorded by Cheryl Lynn, Syreeta, Freddie Hubbard, and Bo Diddley. He co-wrote a jazz instrumental featured in the HBO movie *The Rat Pack* and a funk tune for the Universal film *Undercover Brother*. Cat was commissioned by Opera Pacific to write a children's operetta *The Not So Great Escape,* which was performed in schools throughout Southern California. Cat has released an indie CD of ten original tunes *Songs Of Survival And Sweet Surrender.*

You can find out more about Cat and his long creative career at his author website at www.catcohenauthor.com and his music website www.catcohen.c0m. He can be reached at cat@catcohen.com. Find him at facebook.com/davidcatcohen and follow him at twitter.com/davidcatcohen.

"May your cupboard always be full
and your soup bowl never empty."

www.ingramcontent.com/pod-product-compliance
Lightning Source LLC
Chambersburg PA
CBHW071745090426
42738CB00011B/2569